# Transnational Capitalism and Hydropolitics in Argentina

# TRANSNATIONAL CAPITALISM AND HYDROPOLITICS IN ARGENTINA

## The Yacyretá High Dam

Gustavo Lins Ribeiro

*Foreword by Eric R. Wolf*

**University Press of Florida**
*Gainesville*
*Tallahassee*
*Tampa*
*Boca Raton*
*Pensacola*
*Orlando*
*Miami*
*Jacksonville*

Copyright 1994 by the Board of Regents of the State of Florida
Printed in the United States of America on acid-free paper ⊖
All rights reserved
99  98  97  96  95  94      6  5  4  3  2  1

**Library of Congress Cataloging-in-Publication Data**

Ribeiro, Gustavo Lins.
    Transnational capitalism and hydropolitics in Argentina: the
Yacyretá high dam / Gustavo Lins Ribeiro.
        p.      cm.
    Originally presented as the author's thesis (doctoral)—City
University of New York, 1988.
    Includes bibliographical references and index.
    ISBN 0-8130-1280-5
    1. Entidad Binacional Yacyretá.    2. Hydroelectric power
plants—Social aspects—Argentina.    3. Hydroelectric power
plants—Economic aspects—Argentina.    I. Title.
HD9685.A74E587    1994
333.9'14'0982—dc20                                93-33426
                                                   CIP

The University Press of Florida is the scholarly publishing agency
for the State University System of Florida, comprised of Florida
A & M University, Florida Atlantic University, Florida International
University, Florida State University, University of Central Florida,
University of Florida, University of North Florida, University of
South Florida, and University of West Florida.

University Press of Florida
15 Northwest 15th Street
Gainesville, FL 32611

To Julián, my son

# Contents

# Figures

# Foreword

There are certain milestones that mark the growth and maturation of a system of knowledge. They signal points at which accustomed understandings and inherited approaches are applied to new subject matter and to new problems, and as a result completely transform the course of inquiry. Gustavo Lins Ribeiro's study of the emplacement of the Yacyretá Hydroelectric High Dam in northeastern Argentina constitutes such a turning point.

Anthropology first issued from the encounters between strangers along two frontiers, the first between urban elites and peasant folk in their own countrysides, the second between colonists and native peoples in the New World across the oceans. It first seemed necessary to establish that all the seeming strangers were fully human and then to account for the differences in comportment in cultural terms, not in terms of varying biological constitution. Then came the next great challenge: to understand that these culturally learned ways were not forever fixed but that they were changeable, and that one needed to talk to people and observe them in their daily interactions in hamlets, villages, and communities to discover how cultural custom has shaped behavior and behavior in turn has shaped custom. This gave rise to a further realization, that bodies of custom and sequences of behavior were not propagated in isolation but within interethnic systems, and that these interethnic systems were prompted into being and shaped in their courses by wide-ranging economic and political forces. Thus the anthropologists moved gradually from a focus on local happenings to engage ever widening circles of factors and determinants, yet always cognizant of the importance of local reciprocities and understandings to the workings of economic accumulation and the exercise of power on the part of the state.

Now anthropology faces a further challenge, with the recognition that things can indeed happen *in* localities, but through the workings of the "invisible hand" of the market or through the policies of governments, operating in an ecology of governments. These causes do not emanate *from* the localities, yet they are carried forward and mediated through the actions and understandings of people who are brought together in determinate ways, and who will live under the continuing effects of these new social assemblages. More often than not—and this is where the focus of the anthropologist continues to be critical—both the ways in which the new assemblage was brought together and the ways in which it was then deployed will create unpremeditated and unforeseen effects for the manner in which people manage the conditions of their survival and reproduction.

Nowhere is this clearer than in the establishment of the large-scale economic and state enterprises that has accompanied the rise of the modern world system, such as plantations and deep mines, oil fields and transportation grids, industrial complexes and hydroelectric power systems. These do not derive from local or regional grassroots traditions or desires. They generally respond to national or international demands and are put in place in locations or regions selected according to the guiding criteria of some general or abstract strategy or plan. Often such undertakings respond to an ideal of "progress," an ideal that embodies the intention to "redeem" an area from servitude to backwardness and to orient it toward "development." Sometimes for better and sometimes for worse, these projects uproot people and derange their accustomed ways of life in order to lay down a wholly new infrastructure of constraints and opportunities for the targeted participants. At present, such projects proliferate on an ever increasing continental or subcontinental scale, and that increased scale intensifies their requirements and multiplies their effects.

It is this kind of difficult scenario that Ribeiro has decided to explore for us by applying the techniques and perspectives of anthropology, and in the process he has opened up a whole new field of understanding both for us and his science. He examines the history and the ideology of the Yacyretá project. He shows us how different power groups competed for access to and control of the project. He tells us how the required capital was assembled, how technology and organizational knowledge were mobilized, how the components of the labor force were recruited, assembled, and deployed. He also shows us how the social and physical landscape was modified and redesigned to suit the project's needs, and he examines the implications of the rise of a new kind of nomad laborer, the bicho-de-obra, the work-site animal, with a new identity and a new kind of consciousness.

To the extent that Yacyretá represents a new international and transnational phenomenon, this study addresses issues that have become worldwide. In offering us this fine work, Gustavo Lins Ribeiro has also taken a major step in moving anthropology forward toward the realization of its promise as a human science of global concern.

Eric R. Wolf
City University of New York

# Preface

It is common to find biographical reasons underlying a person's interest in a research subject. My family migrated to Brasília in 1961, when the Brazilian federal capital, inaugurated in 1960, was still a large-scale project under construction. As a child, I heard many stories about the "pioneers," people who had come, despite many difficulties, to the isolated hinterlands of the state of Goiás and built Brazil's new capital. Later, I was to write about the history of the construction of Brasília, seen from the point of view of the construction workers (Ribeiro 1980, 1982). These men, living in camps and struggling against all odds, had built the city and were almost invisible actors in the historical accounts that focused on main political figures such as Brazilian president Juscelino Kubitschek or on Oscar Niemeyer and Lúcio Costa, Brasília's architect and planner.

But what started as a contribution to the understanding of the history of a planned city developed into a research project that would last for more than a decade. The study of the construction of Brasília had shown that a large-scale project could be understood as a system that was recurrent in other geographical and historical contexts. Comparison was thus mandatory. Canals (such as Suez and Panamá), railroads, and hydroelectric dams became the comparative basis upon which I constructed the notion of large-scale projects as a form of production (Ribeiro 1985, 1987).

I understand large-scale projects to be structurally connected to the expansion of political and economic systems. They imply gigantic movements of capital and labor, linking a previously relatively isolated region to an integrated market system. The presence of large-scale projects means the transformation of realities oriented mostly by local rationales to realities where an understanding of the intricate articulation of national and international political and economic interests is crucial.

Most anthropologists study changes provoked by outsiders from a local perspective. I arrived at the field of anthropological studies on development by a different road. My trajectory had made clear—and this is one of the main contributions I see of this book—that in order to understand what the developmental drama is, it was necessary to avoid an explanation from a partial standpoint. This recognition placed my work within the large frameworks of studies of the interactions between local and supralocal realities, of how the expansion of a given political economy occurred and what it meant to local people as well as to all major segments involved in the process.

Large-scale infrastructure projects have caused different impacts on local populations, usually located in relatively isolated areas. The dramatic disruptions of the demographic, social, political, economic, and cultural characteristics of indigenous people and peasants, prompted the involvement of anthropologists with the study and assessment of the "social impacts" of the so-called development projects. Increasingly, these professionals began to work for transnational or public corporations as well as multilateral and development agencies, creating, in a temporary or permanent fashion, a new field of action for anthropology. The involvement of these professionals redefined, once more, the discussion about the discipline as an academic or an applied science.

One of my goals in studying "development projects" was to provide knowledge about the causes of the transformations that were being studied in the impact assessment literature. My reasoning was simple. To understand better the impact and consequences of a large development initiative, one needs to understand the ways it is structured. Indeed, many aspects of what happens to local populations that undergo forced resettlement provoked by development projects have to do with the power and institutional arrangements the projects engender, their demographics, their internal ideologies, and the migratory flows they entail.

Large-scale projects had another provocative dimension for a researcher's imagination. They could be delimited as spatial, economic, political, and social realities but could not be totally explained by taking into account only the observable empirical characteristics of these realities. Indeed, large-scale projects have the power to articulate a great number of interest groups strongly marked by the history of their relationships to a given project. A significant part of my effort was, thus, directed toward understanding the formation of these changing arrangements within and around the Yacyretá project.

This is the first anthropological work to study a large-scale infrastructure project from within. Social scientists, regional planners, engineers, diplomats, environmentalists, and other readers may find here insights not only about the characteristics of large-scale development initiatives, but also about major contemporary issues. How do transnational corporations operate at the global, national, and local levels? What are the situations generated by the political and economic field where transnational corporations, state, and multilateral elites interact? How is development to be assessed regarding the people involved with its logic and the local populations targeted by planners?

To address these issues I combined ethnographic description, a classic asset of anthropological inquiry, with anthropological visions on development, economic expansion, and power differentiation, plus a heterodox methodological and theoretical approach of historical and sociological inspiration. I combined the understandings that social actors had of the situations in which they were involved—the "native" perception of social reality that informed "local knowledge"—with a description of the institutions and scenarios where actions unfold over time. This was consistent with my intention not to reduce my study to an analysis of the cold dynamics of political and economic relations. Rather, I wanted to bring to the forefront the people who were involved and who were produced by and producers of these dynamics. I wanted to write a work in which main contemporary theoretical issues could be explored but that could also provide a feeling of real places, circumstances, and people.

Undoubtedly, a large-scale project like the Yacyretá Hydroelectric High Dam is an excellent place to investigate the connections between cutting-edge theoretical preoccupations and empirical reality. It was a great opportunity to see how transnational and national capital of public and private origins became entangled in a context regulated by the elites of nation-states and of multilateral agencies. The unveiling of a pattern of articulation of political and economic interests proved to be highly productive for my analysis. It facilitated an understanding of how an ethnically segmented labor market was structured, creating the project population. It also allowed an understanding of how the lives of social actors that typically migrate within the global circuits were generated by the logic of these massive investments. It equally revealed the dynamics underlying the major development contradiction of these projects: the drainage of the best human and natural resources out of the areas where they are located.

After years of studying a "development project" I, like many researchers in other situations, came to the conclusion that development needed to be reassessed. What does a multibillion-dollar dam mean to the majority of local people living in precarious social and economic conditions? Liberation from their subordinated position? Participation in the modern world as citizens who can consciously choose their destiny? Disruption of culturally informed collective notions? Adhesion to market-oriented ethics and individualistic notions? The questions are manifold and easy to multiply. But there is only one answer: the prevailing model of development needs to change.

A few years ago such a statement would quickly be dismissed as biased. But in an era of ideological transformations this necessity is clear for an increasingly greater number of people placed in different positions of the political spectrum. I intend this work to be a demonstration of why and how, in the context of large-scale infrastructure projects, development as ideology and as economic, technical, and political action, has not been capable of bringing well-being on a sustainable basis for most of the people affected by a huge planned initiative. This is why I do not call them development projects and why I prefer to use the expression "economic expansion."

By choosing what can be considered as a quintessential example of development initiatives, a large-scale project, I could show development's internal contradictions and demonstrate, with first-hand evidence, its limits, flaws, and unintended results. Central to this was my decision to do research with the main segments of the population participating at the Yacyretá project, from its transnational elite to local gauchos, Argentine cowboys transformed into unskilled workers by the many corporations building the dam. Development seemed to me to be a field of political and economic struggle where those players that start the action do it from an advantageous situation. It is, in the last instance, a power game.

But as most games, development also depends on rules. They are established according to the material characteristics of the elements to be articulated, the various possibilities of articulation, the willingness of participants to abide by the rules, their power to change them, and, finally, according to whether those meaningful actors believe it is worthwhile playing the game. These technological, political, and ideological constraints are sociologically and historically determined and need to be considered in order to understand the final arrangement a large-scale project produces.

The world's political economy is undergoing great changes that modify the perceptions and actions of some of the main developmentalist actors. Geographers, economists, political scientists, sociologists, and anthropologists are increasingly dedicating their attention to "the growing integration of the contemporary world." Transnational capitalism, both at the financial and production levels, generates new forces and accelerates the "shrinking of the world" via advancements in the industries of transportation, communication, and information.

Little ethnographic research has been done about the "growing integration of the world." By studying the construction of a major hydroelectric dam, I also intended to show, in a context intimately related to the expansion of transnational capitalism, that to understand a large-scale developmentalist initiative it was necessary to consider the determinations and interactions among several levels of political and economic power (local, regional, national, and international). A large-scale project places several powerful capitalist agencies together: transnational corporations, multilateral and development agencies, national governments, banks, and so on. I coined the term *consortiation* to refer to the economic and political process through which they become associated. A chain of subcontracting that may reach local-level entrepreneurs under the hegemony of national and transnational actors is established by the organizers of the project.

The notion of consortiation is central for an analysis of the integration of the contemporary world from an economic and political perspective. But this integration has also social and cultural implications. The ethnically segmented population of Yacyretá lives in camps, small villages of the world-system, experiencing alterities it would never be exposed to if it were not for the unifying presence of the project. Furthermore, a segment of highly skilled workers, technicians, and professionals is periodically transferred from one project to another by their corporations' world headquarters. These industrial nomads, the inhabitants of large-scale projects' migratory circuits, comprise a transnational population. I thus analyze the construction of a typical transnational identity, that of the "work-site animals" (bichos-de-obra), generated by and for the necessities of transnational corporations.

Anthropologists studying the contemporary world are faced with increasingly complex issues. This book is an effort to contribute to the interpretation of such complexity, keeping in mind at the same time that one of the strongest appeals of an anthropological work is to expose new, exotic, strange—in a word, different—realities that through research and writing become meaningful to other people's lives.

# Acknowledgments

This book was first conceived as a dissertation for the Ph.D. program in anthropology of the Graduate Center of the City University of New York. After the completion of my thesis (1988), I returned to Brazil where, in 1989, I was honored by the National Association of Research and Graduate Studies in the Social Sciences (ANPOCS) with the award for the best doctoral dissertation by a Brazilian author. Consequently, the work was translated into Portuguese and published (Ribeiro 1991).

Although the present version was edited and some modifications were introduced, especially in its introduction and conclusion, it basically reflects my doctoral work. In this connection, I need to recognize the help and support I received from many people during the years that led to this book.

Different persons and institutions made possible my dedication to academic work in the period 1982–88, the years I spent in the United States and Argentina. I am grateful for the support of the Conselho Nacional de Desenvolvimento Científico e Tecnológico (CNPq) (Brazilian Council for Scientific and Technological Development) and the Wenner-Gren Foundation for Anthropological Research. Without the assistance of these institutions the completion of my training, as well as my research in Argentina, would have been impossible.

I could hardly have had a more stimulating and positive dissertation committee. Dr. June Nash was always an inspiring presence with her suggestions and continuous interest on my work. Dr. Daniel Gross, who in 1977 was my professor at the graduate course in anthropology of the University of Brasília, was responsible for my move to New York in 1982 with my family. I was lucky to count on his friendship and the help of his advice at several important times of those academic years. Dr. Eric Wolf gave me constant intellectual support, something a researcher needs when he thinks he is exploring new ground. Thanks to his interest I continued my research on large-scale projects and formulated an abstract notion of them and some of the questions that are being dealt with in this book. It was a pleasure to count on his scholarship and advice on several matters. I also appreciated Dr. Shelton Davis's participation as an external reader. He, together with other colleagues, is presently showing that anthropologists have an important role to play in the world of planning and public policy.

From the point of view of the institutions that I studied, there are controversial points that expose either the characteristics of power arrangements related to Yacyretá or issues that are part of the project's reality but have never been previously presented in a systematic manner. It should be clear that I do not envisage these questions as particular to the Yacyretá project. I hope it will be understood that a major purpose of this book is to show that large-scale projects involve a complex totality of human phenomena.

I wish to thank all the persons that helped me enter and understand the complexity of the Yacyretá project. I was glad to count on the support of people at different levels of the various institutions I researched in Buenos Aires, Posadas (Misiones), and Ituzaingó (Corrientes). Without their help and understanding I would not have been able to do this research. A large-scale project is a highly institutionalized environment, one where a researcher needs to be granted permission to develop the work. In this sense, I am particularly endebted to Entidad Binacional Yacyretá because, despite the fact that the presence of an independent researcher is anxiety causing, it allowed for the normal unfolding of my work. For me this was a permanent indication of how strongly democracy is valued in contemporary Argentina.

In Posadas I was glad to be accepted by the Department of Anthropology of the Universidad Nacional de Misiones as visiting researcher. I benefited from the experience of several colleagues who have worked either on

Yacyretá itself or on the colonization of Misiones and Corrientes. I thank them all through the figure of Ana Maria Gorosito Kramer. Marcelo Larricq, a student in the department, helped me collect data on the civil construction unions in Misiones and Corrientes. Dr. Leopoldo J. Bartolomé went out of his way to make me feel comfortable during my field research in Misiones and Corrientes. I thank him, Graciela, and the children for their warm hospitality and friendship.

In Buenos Aires I could meet and discuss my research subject and Argentine social reality with several colleagues working at the Universidad de Buenos Aires. I thank Carlos Herrán, Maurício Boivin, Hugo Rattier, Ana Rosato, Federico Neiburg, Raúl Diaz, Ivy Radovich, and, especially, Rosana Guber. Unfortunately, my gratitude to Dr. Esther Hermitte has to be a posthumous homage. She died in 1990, leaving behind a life dedicated to the growth of anthropology in Argentina.

I was also fortunate to have met with members of the Centro de Estudios Urbanos y Regionales (CEUR) that were developing their own research on contemporary large-scale Argentine projects. I appreciated my discussions with Elsa Laurelli, Alícia Vidal, and Fernando Brunstein. Finally, in Buenos Aires I had the privilege to discuss my research on large-scale projects in a course I taught at the Instituto de Desarrollo Económico y Social (IDES). I thank Getúlio Steinbach for having honored me on the invitation to expound my ideas in such a prestigious institution.

In New York I counted on the unmistakable support of my friends and colleagues in CUNY's Ph.D. program, Chris Leonard, Lígia Simonian, Luís Loyola, and Joe Heyman. Jonathan Poor has helped me in ways hard to acknowledge. His support on different matters made possible the completion of my dissertation within a reasonable time frame. The same is true for David Elliot's help. I must also acknowledge Dr. Scott Guggenheim and Dr. Judith Freidenberg for their comments and suggestions on some chapters.

Yacyretá Means *The Moon Land* in Guarani

# 1 Introduction

The town of Altamira, in Brazilian Amazonia, had never seen so many Indians, activists, politicians, superstars, and cameras. It was February 1989, and a meeting organized by Brazilian and international nongovernmental organizations was being held to protest Kararaô, a major dam planned to be constructed on the Xingú River. A Kayapó woman, in front of the world media, threatened with a machete an executive of Eletronorte, the state-owned company responsible for the generation and distribution of energy in Brazil's Amazonia. At the same time that this woman was defending her land and people from the forced resettlement to be caused by Kararaô's huge reservoir, thousands of people were in the streets of several European and American cities protesting the environmental and social impacts of the hydroelectric dams to be built in the Amazon River basin.

Although not all of the many dams planned or under construction worldwide have the same visibility of those of the Amazon region, there has been a growing global concern about the construction of large-scale projects because of their negative effects on the environment and local populations. The social sciences could not be immune to these realities. In fact, the involvement of anthropologists and other social scientists with so-called development projects began to intensify in the 1970s when powerful multilateral agencies, such as the World Bank, recognized that local populations were not enjoying the benefits these projects are sup-

1

posed to bring. Consequently, "social impact assessment" has become a flourishing field, one where researchers have produced a literature almost exclusively dedicated to the analysis of forced resettlement.

Following a different path, I considered that to understand the impacts of a so-called development project, it is necessary to know their causes. I decided to study a major dam, the largest under construction in Latin America, the Yacyretá Hydroelectric High Dam, an Argentine-Paraguayan project on the Paraná River. This book contributes to the understanding of a development initiative that impacts local populations. This book shows the internal organization of a large-scale project, its political and economic power, its settlement patterns and social life, as well as the associated migratory flows and social changes. Besides creating information and analytical tools for the understanding of large-scale projects throughout the world, I aimed at addressing crucial theoretical problems such as the growing integration of the contemporary world and the different meanings that development may have for social actors.

Although this book contains some of the same material found in my previous works, it asks different and broader questions provoked by the maturation of the research subject and its location in a larger theoretical framework. My work on the construction of Brasília (Ribeiro 1980, 1982) led me to formulate the concept of a form of production typical of large-scale projects carried out in isolated areas. I wanted to develop a framework on a level of abstraction comparable to anthropological discussions about plantations. After doing a comparative analysis, I concluded that there was enough evidence to propose that large-scale projects constituted a form of production that has recurrent and discrete characteristics, and that they are linked to the expansion of economic systems (Ribeiro 1985, 1987).

But, when I began to develop such an abstract framework, I also realized that although I was aware of the complexity of institutional arrangements and of the intricate multiple articulations of power groups around and within a large-scale project, I needed a better understanding of their importance. It was also clear that there was a need for a more detailed picture of the relationships between social actors operating at the international and national levels and their relationships to the populations actually engaged in the construction projects. Large-scale projects seemed to be an ideal unit of analysis for an ethnographic exploration of some of the most interesting contemporary anthropological questions, such as the growing interdependency of international, national, regional, and local realities; the emergence of transnational populations; the formation of ethnically segmented labor markets; the uneven distribution of political and economic power within social systems; and the discussion of development as ideology. Of particular interest was how the different levels of integration defined by the dynamics and interpenetrations of international, national, regional, and local realities unfolded within a large-scale project, an environment where the importance of these connections is self-evident.

I then focused on the internal population of Yacyretá, defined to encompass all segments directly active in the total labor force of the project: from the people of the local population recruited to participate in the construction effort to the technical and managerial segments of the project placed at the construction site or at regional and national corporate headquarters. This focus was congruent with my conception of large-scale projects as a form of production, and at the same time it avoided the problems of a reified notion of community. I was not so much concerned with actors' residential locations, but with their power of intervening in the lives and directions of the population of the Yacyretá project. The project was thus clearly delimited as a power structure that could not be understood by a single locational reference.

The initial intention of empirically locating and delimiting the social networks that actually connect the different levels of power and social agency proved, nonetheless, to be marked both by residual empiricist overtones and by a misunderstanding of the functioning of bureaucratic structures. Indeed, since Yacyretá is a project that unfolds in specific historical moments and attracts a variety of power groups by its political and economic importance, I soon realized that it would not be possible to trace all the webs of social networks that dominated the project's entire production process; there are simply too many of them in operation at any given moment. To trace their structuring, their relationships within the project as well as with other groups external to the project (lobby groups, for instance) is perhaps logically possible, but would involve research work that, even for a team of researchers, would either prove to be endless or to duplicate information easily available in other data sources, such as the discourses of qualified informants and historical analysis.

Furthermore, much of the continuity between the different levels of integration does not rest on the existence of social networks that interact freely and are open to interpersonal manipulation. On the contrary, social networks in a large-scale project operate in an institutionalized environment. This is an environment in which a bureaucratic-institutional structure guarantees the continuation of the project over time, in a manner *relatively* independent of the interplay of power groups situated in various hierarchical positions.

This fundamental characteristic of the object of research led me to analyze the institutional setting of the Yacyretá Hydroelectric project, a setting constituted by public, transnational, and national corporations developing different roles within the project. In chapter 2, I propose the existence of an "institutional triangle" formed by (1) the public corporation that owns the project, the Entidad Binacional Yacyretá, EBY (Yacyretá Binational Entity); (2) the consultant firm, CIDY (Consultores Internacionales de Yacyretá); and (3) the main contractor, ERIDAY (Empresas Reunidas Impregilo–Dumez y Asociados para Yacyretá). Both CIDY and ERIDAY were set up by transnational and national corporations. To understand the three internal organizations and their mutual relationships, the analysis of the dynamics of different levels of integration needs to consider the relations between the state, national, and international firms. Given the fact that the Yacyretá project has an institutional history that began in 1958, a historical approach was mandatory. This approach proved to be useful in disentangling the complex relations that developed with the project over time by different power groups.

For a study of the interaction between international and national levels, it became evident that there was a crucial institutionalized arena in which the economic and political power groups defined their participation in the project: the bidding processes of the major contracts related to the execution of the construction work. In chapter 3 there is an analysis of the ways in which the main civil works contract and the turbines contract (the major segments in the construction of a hydroelectric dam) were awarded. This analysis shows how important local-level phenomena, such as the internal composition of the population directly engaged in the construction of Yacyretá, were inextricably related to the dynamics of the international and national levels. Indeed, the present demographic configuration of Ituzaingó, the department in the northeastern Argentine province of Corrientes where the major civil works have been placed, is marked by the constitution of the construction consortium that is building the dam. The lead firms of this consortium are Italian- and French-based corporations. This is why there can be found a foreign population composed mostly of Italians and French and not by Koreans or North Americans.

The analysis of the bidding processes also allowed me to define a process that I call *consortiation*. Consortiation is a notion useful for making sense of the political and economic aspects of the relationships between different levels of integration as they occur within large-scale projects. It also enables one to relate the local and regional development process to the more general process of transnational capitalist accumulation in which the flow of capital is dominated by social actors operating at higher levels.

The analysis of different levels of integration called for an equal emphasis on local reality. In chapter 4, I focused on the local setting, delineating the different scenarios where the social actions of project-related groupings unfolded. Here again, the organizing powers of the Yacyretá project were manifested in the settlement pattern of the area. The internal organization of the production process was mirrored by social life in the different residential areas of the project. Furthermore, the analysis demonstrates not only the relatively powerless position of the *Ituzain-gueños* as compared with the powerful structure that came to encompass their backyard, but shows how the predominance of higher levels of integration (national and international) affected in observable ways the daily management of the project within the territory of construction. Indeed, both Argentine officials working for the public corporation that owns the project and foreign managers working for private firms had to retreat to national or international decision-making centers when more delicate decisions had to be reached. There was little doubt where the main power centers where located.

Chapter 5 is about the intricate relationships of labor market formation and differentiation and the several migratory labor flows structuring the population of the Yacyretá project. In order to gather data that would allow me to follow the complexity of these issues I had to make a crucial decision during field research concerning labor and class relations. The Yacyretá project has been marked by a history of political confrontations among workers, private corporations, and governmental agencies. This is especially true for the Argentine workers that count on a powerful union structure. That does not mean that the Paraguayan workers have not engaged in organized movements. Given the then-authoritarian nature of the Paraguayan regime, though, workers' political activities were subject to restrictions and control. In December 1986, for instance, seven workers (one Uruguayan, three Argentines, and three Paraguayans) that were participating in a union assembly, were arrested by Paraguayan authorities (see *El Clarín,* Buenos Aires, December 7, 1986; *El Litoral,* Corrientes, December 13, 1986). Besides the fact that they were kept in prison for several weeks, there were also reports of physical abuses committed by Paraguayan authorities (*La Razón,* Buenos Aires, January 24, 1987). Strikes were also frequent. At least one of these strikes involved the occupation and control of the construction site by workers, heightening the tension in the project's territory. On at least two ocasions, workers demonstrated not only at the local level, in Ituzaingó, but also in Buenos Aires where union leaders from the project area camped in front of the national congress and fasted for several days to gather national attention.

Focusing on class struggle might have revealed interesting characteristics of the labor-capital relationships in Yacyretá, but would have led to a terrain already thoroughly studied by social scientists, economists, and historians, rather than toward a better understanding of large-scale projects. Instead, I chose to characterize the migratory circuit permanently related to large-scale projects as a strategic way to understand those projects in relation to international and national processes of capitalist expansion. Moreover, focusing on the migration circuit could point to a dynamic conception of a project's labor market segmentation. For these reasons, I paid substantial attention to the description and analysis of what I call the large-scale project migratory circuit and its typical participant, the bicho-de-obra, or work-site animal. Chapter 5 ends with a discussion on labor market segmentation in which I show how the market is structured by the labor needs of corporations and by migratory processes, as well as the social changes associated with these imperatives.

This book is strongly directed toward an interpretation of the present state of integration of the world system. But the scenario where the research was carried out was also highly conducive to the discussion of development issues, a matter of great importance when what is at stake are the relationships between powerful large-scale projects and local populations. In the last chapter I thus turn to a broader consideration of development as ideology and to the reasons why a large-scale project such as the Yacyretá Dam can hardly be defined as a development project.

In the next section, I will situate the development of my arguments by highlighting the influences that are pervasive in the unfolding of my reasoning throughout this work. I do not pretend to offer an epistemology of the different theoretical issues involved in the particular fields of anthropological studies to which I will refer. In fact, the vocabulary and part of my reasonings do indicate a certain eclecticism. I agree with the assessment of Marcus and Fischer that "a period of experimentation is characterized by eclecticism, the play of ideas free of authoritative paradigms, critical and reflexive views of subject matter, openness to diverse influences embracing whatever seems to work in practice, and tolerance of uncertainty about a field's direction and of incompleteness in some of its projects" (1986, x).

## Am I an Anthropologist? Anthropology and Large-Scale Projects

A question I was frequently asked in the process of working on this subject—especially during field research—was whether I was an anthropologist. The most informed of the persons trying to understand my work would think that I was doing research on the impact of the construction of the Yacyretá Hydroelectric High Dam on the populations of the northeastern Argentine provinces of Corrientes and Misiones. Less-informed persons, still with some idea of what anthropology is, thought I was doing archaeological research or, surprisingly, looking for bones, for fossils. For others, I was simply the "anthro-lo-pogist," not the anthropo-lo-gist. I guess it did not really matter for them what I was doing. But, whatever the level of information of the person puzzled by the presence of an anthro(lo)po(lo)gist doing research at a large-scale project on the border of Argentina and Paraguay, I had to take seriously the constant reiteration of the question of who I was. Indeed, it involved not only a perception of anthropology as a discipline, but also a certain curiosity about what an anthropologist does in such a setting as a construction project, or how an anthropologist contributes to the understanding of a large-scale project.

There is no single and easy way of answering these questions. I shall briefly address the ways in which an anthropologist studying a large-scale project is directly, or indirectly, responding to topics that have always been of central concern to anthropology. There are at least four different broad anthropological traditions that bear immediately on the study of large-scale projects: (1) the analysis of economic expansion; (2) the preoccupation with understanding the relationships between different levels of integration; (3) the emergence of "development anthropology," a relatively recent advent in the history of the discipline; and (4) Karl Wittfogel's thesis of the hydraulical state.

## Economic Expansion

The study of economic expansion, that is, the study of the incorporation of new populations and territorial areas into a broader economic system, has always been present—explicitly or not—in the development of anthropology. Even functionalist anthropologists hoping to contour sui generis social isolates would agree that the very presence of an ethnographer in the most isolated indigenous societies is an index that a regional, national, or international socioeconomic system is expanding into an area previously tangential to the broader system. Others in the history of the discipline who have never been totally convinced by the argument of self-contained social isolates have argued constantly for the need for analyzing societies, social groups, and modes of production in *relationship* to each other *and* as part of a larger whole. Furthermore, this whole is envisaged as a system, or to put it in another way, as parts of intimately interconnected and mutually informing segments of a broader reality.

There are efforts, in the anthropological literature, that cope with the need to understand the "internal" characteristics of an organized population and how its relations to other populations imply social change. The efforts to understand socioeconomic-political and cultural "types," such as plantations, are highly representative of this trend. In classic anthropological discussions on this topic, such as those found in Palerm and Rubin (1959), at the same time that plantations are analyzed as unique forms of organizing a population to attain certain economic goals, they are also related to the economic system that creates them as specific arrangements and that defines their economic goals. These and other anthropological works have made clear that the claim for culturally and socially sui generis populations is as mythical as the belief in a pure race (see, for instance, Harris 1964).

The encounter of endogenous and exogenous social processes has been of constant interest for anthropologists because they occur in settings where different conceptions about the reproduction of social life are involved. Indeed, the analysis of internal characteristics and external forces seems to be related to a fundamental tension that permeates anthropology as a whole; that is, anthropologists are frequently coping with paradoxes that, sometimes in their appearances of logical irreducibility, seem to be permanent. Thus, to understand the "other," anthropologists make efforts to neutralize their ethnocentrism. At the same time, anthropologists cannot deny the particularities of the cultures they study, but need to place them in a universal framework. Thus, not everything can be explained in terms of internal characteristics or of external influences. An either-or approach in anthropology seems to be doomed to give way to a perspective that cannot attribute a priori value to one or another set of characteristics, factors, or determinations. This might well be one of the reasons why methodology is such a sphinx in anthropology. This is also the reason why field research remains so important for anthropologists, as the main basis for their contributions to theoretical discussions.

But, and returning to the center of the discussion, processes of economic expansion have usually implied an imbalance of power in interethnic contact. At this level, it is useful to point to some of the contributions made by Brazilian anthropologists. Indeed, the works of Darcy Ribeiro (see, for instance, Ribeiro 1970) and Roberto Cardoso de Oliveira (1967, 1976) have opened a path where the study of an indigenous population living within Brazil's territory was clearly considered in terms of the relations between those populations and the expansion of that country's economic frontier. Otávio Velho (1972, 1976) is another example of an analyst related to this interpretative trend that evolved to an overall formulation on the importance of the "moving frontier" in Brazil.

Cardoso de Oliveira's (1967, 1976) notions of "interethnic friction" and of an "interethnic system" have consistently pointed to the need of considering local indigenous populations in relation to the different conflicts developed with an expanding Brazilian society. This framework not only calls for an understanding of the effects of expanding economies on local populations, but also makes explicit the uneven distribution of power in the encounters among different ethnic groups. The latter might be the reason why Cardoso de Oliveira's conceptions were acknowledged as a useful paradigm in the interpretation of interethnic conflict in general (Gross 1985). In this connection, my focus on the uneven distribution of power that occurs when different populations encounter each other is consistent with a trend in Brazilian anthropology that relates ethnicity to power conflict. As we shall see, in Yacyretá, local-level populations face the impact caused by the needs of Argentina's national political economy in a context where ethnic and regional identities are an issue.

Evidently, the idea that social change is embedded in a larger grid of unequal distribution of political and economic power is not exclusive to Brazilian anthropologists. Perhaps the most elaborate development of this conception is Eric Wolf's (1982) book *Europe and the People without History*. In this work, the connections and interpenetrations of human populations are analyzed against the background of the history of capitalist development. Wolf simultaneously stresses the diversity of the different works of capitalist expansion and its underlying historical pattern: the accumulation of capital on a global scale. Such a framework calls for accounts capable of dealing with the heterogeneity of social, economic, political, and cultural forms without disregarding the homogenizing forces that have historically been creating newly segmented social realities and an increasingly integrated world. I hope that the analysis of the Yacyretá project will help show how diverse populations, with different backgrounds, are put into the same social reality by a happening that is directly related to the dynamics of the world system and of the national political economy. My study contributes to an ongoing discussion within anthropology on how the complexities of social and cultural systems are to be conceptualized.

## Levels of Integration

It is almost common knowledge in contemporary anthropology to admit to a world of "increased interdependence." For June Nash "what distinguishes the present interest in the world scope of anthropology is the paradigm of integration of all people and cultures within a world capitalist system" (1981, 393). The need for frameworks and theoretical approaches that account for the increasing complexity and interdependence of the world is particularly challenging for anthropologists since a local social reality, the traditional ethnographic focus of the discipline, cannot be reduced to a world system reality, or vice versa. Frequently, the solution for this type of problem has been sought in the analysis of part-whole relationships or in the intersections between what is conceived as an international system and a national, regional, or local one. Sydel Silverman considered that

> most attempts to tackle this problem have been concerned primarily with those parts which are localized social systems, or communities, interdependent with though analytically separable from the whole, a national social system. The community and national levels of sociocultural integration of Steward (1955, 43–63), the discussion of tensions between pueblo and state by Pitt-Rivers (1954, 202–10), the community-oriented groups and nation oriented-groups of Wolf (1956), and the local roles and national roles of Pitkin (1959) are only a few examples of this recurring contrast, the social analogue of the great-tradition/little tradition approach to complex cultures. Such a model immediately sets the task of formulating the interaction between the two systems. (Silverman 1965, 172)

Apparently, discussions in the 1950s and 1960s were primarily concerned with local- and national-level relationships. The international level would be a later addition to this type of discussion among anthropologists. However, to frame these questions either in terms of "articulations" or "levels" may duly stress overlapping and part-whole relationships but fail to emphasize the simultaneous and significantly condensed character of the interpenetrations of international, national, regional, and local processes. It was a combination of a processual and an analytical vision that guided my inquiry on the Yacyretá project. In doing so, I was following a line of inquiry that informs notions such as "levels of sociocultural integration" and "multilineal development" elaborated more than forty years ago by Julian Steward (see Steward 1950, 1979). He wanted to show the interconnectedness of different levels of integration without losing the internal specificities of each level and without implying that a given evolutionary path is the only avenue along which all socioeconomic, political, and cultural forms travel through time. Steward's conceptions are representative of a long-standing endeavor to conceptualize different instances that potentially or concretely, individually or collectively, in a single moment or over time, intervene in the structuring of social reality and, therefore, in the agency of social actors.

Steward's work indicates that anthropologists and other social scientists were not immobilized by the overwhelming, sometimes apparently chaotic diversity of human social reality and its relationships to factors bounded by local and nonlocal realities. Indeed, anthropologists continue to seek regularities and abstractions capable of interpreting social life in a holistic way, without blotting out the persisting diversity of human experience.

But, it could be asked, why is it important to return to these questions? One strong reason is that they remain important for the development of contemporary anthropology. The continuing influence of these discussions is recognizable in the works of anthropologists that formulate analysis where international, national, and local levels are considered (see Nash 1979, 174). Today these questions are almost taken for granted without having triggered the creation of a methodology and approach for the analysis of contemporary anthropological objects. Undoubtedly, anthropologists will have to deal more constantly with this kind of issue since reality increasingly fuses local, regional, national, and international processes. As time passes, these questions will be even more relevant for the understanding of social reality.

Having to weigh and assess the differential importance for social actors of these different ''levels of integration'' significantly increases the burden of research and scholarship contemporary anthropologists have to carry. It may well be another index of the overall ambition of a discipline that was once called ''the science of man.''

## Development Anthropology

The nature of contemporary capitalist expansion has increasingly called the attention for the role of ''development projects'' on a global scale. Scudder and Colson noted that this is an ''era of national development plans that call for the construction of dams and other major engineering projects'' (1982, 268). Kathleen Murphy considered the 1970s as the decade of ''macroproject development in the Third World'' when over 900 projects were begun and at least 600 more were on the drawing boards (1983, xv). Billion-dollar projects are not rare; the costs of twenty top projects selected by Murphy range from U.S.$5 billion to U.S.$21 billion (1983, xvii, 6,7). According to her sample, investments in the 1970s represented more than U.S.$500 billion, and each project employed more than 10,000 persons (Murphy 1983, vii, xv).

In my own efforts to conceptualize large-scale projects as a form of production, I focused on their qualitative dimensions rather than on their quantitative aspects (Ribeiro 1985, 1987). These projects are undertakings that typically involve complex relationships between financial and industrial capital and nation-states in different world areas. The evident disruption and potential or virtual disasters these massive investments imply for local populations prompted the involvement of anthropologists in the study and assessment of their impact. The social impact assessment is a growing field in which anthropologists participate in significant ways. Indeed, from the pioneering and now classic study of Elizabeth Colson (1971) to the formulation of a general framework of analysis of forced resettlement (Scudder and Colson 1982), the topic grew so consistently as to create a new subfield of the discipline, development anthropology.

Studies in the social impact assesment literature have shown that projects are not monolithic carriers of development for all social classes, segments, or ethnic groups involved or affected by them (Colson 1971, 3, 140ff.; Duqué 1980; Partridge et al. 1982; Bartolomé 1984). Indeed, examples of hydroelectric projects such as Volta (Ghana), Kariba (Zimbabwe), Tucuruí and Sobradinho (Brazil), and the Pick-Sloan Plan (United States)—to mention but a few—indicate that projects favor large national and international economic concentrations to the detriment of local populations (Payer 1982, 256–66; IBASE 1983; Sigaud 1986; Lawson 1982).

In contemporary anthropological literature, most works are concerned with the *effects* of large-scale projects (mainly the construction of hydroelectric plants with the artificial lakes they create) on local populations (e.g., Aspelin and Santos 1981; Aspelin 1982; Hansen and Oliver-Smith 1982). Although the emphasis on "the social consequences of innovation" is traditional within the discipline (Dalton 1971, 11), this time anthropologists are being placed at the core of some discussions related to world and national planning policies. Policy shifts in major international financing agencies that promote "development projects" represented a new demand on anthropology and prompted the appearance and growth of development anthropology. The major task of the development anthropologist is to "enhance benefits and mitigate negative consequences for the human communities involved in and affected by development efforts" (Partridge and Warren 1984, 1; see also Hoben 1982). At this level, anthropology is apparently caught in a dilemma. While it has a "history of involvement with development projects'' (Partridge and Warren 1984, 5), "the contribution of anthropology to development planning and the response of development programs to anthropological methods and theory have been marginal at best" (Hoben 1984, 9).

The increasing integration of the contemporary world and the important roles that large-scale projects play in this process may signify that anthropologists are facing again the difficult questions about the relationship between the practice of anthropology as an academic discipline and as an applied science. Contemporary development projects are responsible for social changes among native populations that are comparable to the effects caused by plantations, mines, railroad construction, and other concentrated capital investments. Despite the fact that the relationship between anthropologists and development projects raises interesting new theoretical and practical challenges for the discipline, what the involvement of anthropologists in development projects means has not yet received systematic public discussion. Such a discussion would potentially raise new ethical and political questions. Indeed, perhaps for the first time in the history of the discipline, anthropologists have direct or indirect access to world-system decision-making centers (Cernea 1988, 1989). The relationship between anthropology and planned development is currently the subject of a developing and stimulating debate (see Robertson 1986, for an elaborated statement on this issue).

This book should also be read as a contribution to these escalating debates about how development projects are to be assessed. The material stresses the power structures associated with large-scale projects, and calls attention to the ways in which these power structures are affected, and in turn, how they affect the wider distribution of power in the political and economic scenario that surrounds them. I hope this book will furnish data and conceptions that have not yet been put forward by anthropologists or by other independent researchers.

## Karl Wittfogel's Thesis of the Hydraulical State

Among the several anthropological studies I am considering as directly or indirectly related to a discussion of large-scale projects, perhaps Karl Wittfogel's book (1957) on the relationships between large hydraulic works and the emergence of the first states seems to be most tangential to my own. Whether hydraulic works give rise to the state or the concentration of power has been a prerequisite for the construction of water works has been a hotly debated issue in and out of academe (see Bloch 1977, 1985, 113–14; Wolf 1982, 403; Palerm 1973, 324; Godelier 1977, 254–55). Indeed, the relationship between centralized political power and the capacity for pooling labor to carry out great works has long been perceived. Ibn Khaldun, the Arab historian (1332–1406), considered that in the context of urbanization, political centralization, the development both of technology and the division of labor: "Only strong royal authority is able to construct large cities and high monuments. . . . [The size of monuments] is proportionate to the importance of [the various dynasties]. The construction of cities can be achieved only by united effort, great numbers, and the cooperation of workers. When the dynasty is large and far-flung, workers are brought together from all regions and their labour is employed in a common effort" (Khaldun 1969, 265).

My consideration of Wittfogel does not mean that I draw from his work as a model to be applied for the understanding of the origins of the state. His work, however, calls attention to a question that is central to the comprehension of any large-scale project: the relationships between managerial elites, state planners, and the concentration of politico-administrative power in the hands of organizers and controllers of large labor forces.

One possible reading of Wittfogel's work might connect it with discussions that are not unfamiliar to anthropologists but are more frequently carried out by archaeologists, geographers, and urban or regional planners who are concerned with central place theories or regional analysis. At this level, careful consideration is given to the restructuring power exercised by large-scale localized production and trading activities over local and regional systems. Although this is not the focus of the present book, some of the analysis developed in chapters 4 and 5 address questions that are relevant to this type of discussion.

Raising this issue is important because a holistic analysis of large-scale projects implies a complex interface with other disciplines. Large-scale projects are commonly denominated *development projects,* a fact that includes them immediately within the development-underdevelopment literature. The interdisciplinary character of the analysis of development is currently widely recognized. For instance, in the preface of a "textbook for undergraduates in development studies and in economics, politics, sociology, and history courses where development issues are the primary concern,'' Ray Bromley and Gavin Kitching, the series editors, stated the following: "The nature of the subject matter has forced both scholars and practitioners to transcend the boundaries of their own disciplines whether these be social sciences, like economics, human geography or sociology, or applied sciences such as agronomy, plant biology or civil engineering. It is now a conventional wisdom of development studies that development problems are so multi-faceted and complex that *no* single discipline can hope to encompass them, let alone offer solutions" (Kitching 1982).

Naturally, any interdisciplinary approach implies a reconnaissance of the limitations of an individual researcher. But the necessity of confronting various theoretical and practical problems is, in last instance, a response to the characteristics of an object such as the Yacyretá Dam that is highly marked by multidisciplinary conceptions and practices. I hope that this book will represent a step toward an increasing awareness of the need for interdisciplinary research on large-scale projects.

Relating to an interdisciplinary approach also entails several risks. There is, for instance, the risk of sounding naive to specialists in other disciplines who have different training backgrounds. There is also the danger of sounding strange for anthropologists. In this case some naiveté and freshness—and I do not think that these can be completely transformed into crystallized or formal techniques—are what make the anthropological approach unique and powerful. Perhaps the strength of the anthropological imagination relies on a sort of pretended and actual educated ignorance that the anthropologist learns to live with in the field site.

## Doing Research on the Yacyretá Hydroelectric High Dam

One of my central contentions is that to understand the characteristics of development projects and the social changes they cause, it is necessary to comprehend the variety of institutions and social actors involved in their planning and execution. In this work on Yacyretá, I was guided by this perspective. While doing field research, *everything* was important, from the role and importance of the World Bank, the transnational corporations, the nation-states involved in the geopolitics of the upper Paraná River to the history of Ituzaingó, the department of the province of Corrientes where the dam is being built, with its cattle-ranching past, its gauchos (cowboys), and its perception of national-level politics marked by the project, an economic enterprise where the power of the central government in Buenos Aires is self-evident.

To understand the different power capabilities of international, national, regional, and local social actors in relation to the same recognizable structure, the Yacyretá project, I had to develop a vision from the Argentine headquarters of the project located in Buenos Aires—a major arena of articulation of national and international interests. Then I had to contrast that vision with regional and local perspectives as they unfolded in field research scenarios drawn from Posadas, the capital city of Misiones— where a regional office important to the project was located—and from the area of construction in Ituzaingó (see fig. 1). This "multilocale ethnography" (Marcus and Fischer 1986, 90–95) helped me to avoid empiricist and functionalist notions of community and also to address ethnographically the central issue of relationships among levels.

The field research for this book was carried out from December 1985 to March 1987. Given the characteristics of my subject, I had to use diverse research techniques as well as look for varied data sources. This work thus combines data collected with different methodological and theoretical tools. It is the result of a historical analysis of archival material, an analysis of quantitative descriptions of the population engaged in the project, and an analysis of open-ended and formal interviews carried out in several cities and ethnographic contexts, with social actors occupying various levels of positions within the hierarchical structure of the project.

In Buenos Aires, where the Argentine headquarters of Yacyretá is located, I did both open-ended and formal interviews with officials, mostly engineers, of the public corporation that owns the project, the Entidad Binacional Yacyretá, or EBY (Yacyretá Binational Entity). I also spent several months doing archival research in the documentation center of the project, especially on a comprehensive collection of Argentine and Paraguayan newspaper clippings on the Yacyretá project, which covered the period 1969–87. This collection proved to be fundamental to the development of a historical understanding of the project.

The use of newspapers as sources of information is highly complicated and entails different decisions on the part of a researcher to appraise the quality of data. There are two pervasive problems with this type of source. First, censorship of information is typical in authoritarian regimes such as

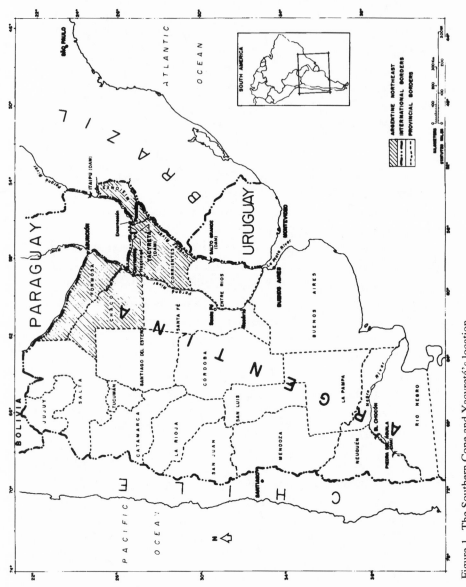

Figure 1. The Southern Cone and Yacyretá's location

that of the Paraguayan under General Stroessner and the several dictator-ships in recent Argentine history. The second problem, which seems to be even more pervasive and is apparently independent of political regimes, is the manipulation of information for political and economic purposes. I constantly checked the controversial data coming out of the Paraguayan and Argentine press against other sources, especially qualified informants. When this could not be done, either the information was not used or was used with a warning contextualizing it. Sometimes, knowledge of evident manipulation of the media was more important than the news itself. Comparing what was published in Asunción with what was published in Buenos Aires proved to be revealing since there were several differences between Paraguayan and Argentine interests.

In Posadas, Misiones, the EBY has an important regional headquarters, responsible primarily for the resettlement of the population of the city that is going to be affected by the filling of Yacyretá's reservoir. Since Posadas is not only the largest Argentine city close to the project site, about 100 kilometers, but also a regional center, in this segment of the field research I focused primarily on issues of regional development, especially on what impact the project might have on the dynamics of the local and regional productive forces. I gathered printed material on this question and carried on open-ended interviews on the relationship between the project and the region with officials linked to the EBY. I also interviewed officials of the province of Misiones working at the interface between national power represented by EBY and provincial political power. In addition, I inter-viewed local formal and informal leaders. I visited one of the first housing projects constructed by EBY as part of its resettlement program. It is already inhabited by people who previously resided in the area of the future reservoir. I also went to the river areas where the bulk of the Posadeña population to be resettled is still living (on the impact of resettlement in Posadas, see Bartolomé 1984). Finally, in Posadas, I discussed the regional importance of Yacyretá with professors and students of the Universidad Nacional de Misiones who have been following the history of the project and its impact on the city and region.

During 1986, I alternately spent time in Buenos Aires and in the town of Ituzaingó, province of Corrientes. This proved to be a fruitful procedure because it allowed me to check national and international issues in light of data obtained at the local level, and vice versa. In Ituzaingó I interviewed officials working for the EBY as well as employees of the main contractor, such as engineers and technicians, and of the consultant firm. At this point, my research focused on the people who worked at the departments responsible for the formation and control of Yacyretá's labor market. I gathered substantial qualitative and quantitative data on the growth of Yacyretá's labor force.

I was also interested in differentiating the groups working for the project in terms of their hierarchical positions within the corporations for which they worked. I thus interviewed professionals (engineers, geologists, architects, and lawyers), technicians, and workers. To develop a varied perspective of workers' visions, I interviewed workers of different trades, leaders of the local union as well as nonunionized workers. Given the important role Europeans play in the project's management, I dedicated a substantial part of my attention to comprehending the internal characteristics of that segment.

Another important component of this research meant gaining an understanding of the population that lived in Ituzaingó before the arrival of the Yacyretá project. Following the overall pattern orienting my field research, I gathered census data on the evolution of Ituzaingó's population and carried out open-ended and formal interviews with social actors occupying diverse positions within the town's system of social stratification. I interviewed local politicians affiliated with different political parties, landholders, gauchos, entrepreneurs, workers, and squatters living on the town's periphery.

Finally, in Ituzaingó I made several visits to the work site and to various labor camps and mess halls in order to survey the living and working conditions as well as to develop a sense of the magnitude of the construction project and its progress.

Given the fact that the Yacyretá Hydroelectric High Dam is a binational project, there was also a need to grasp the Paraguayan perspective. I soon realized that it would be practically impossible for a single researcher to do justice to the special characteristics of the Paraguayan viewpoint. Besides the material and time limitations I faced, I sensed that prolonged anthropological research on a sensitive issue such as the country's largest project under construction would not be feasible in Paraguay. Notwithstanding, I could, however, gain some understanding of Paraguay's position using, for instance, material on the dam in the Paraguayan press. Furthermore, a few times I visited the residential infrastructure of the project on the Paraguayan side of the work site, near the town of Ayolas. There I interviewed officials working for EBY, focusing specifically on issues that could clarify Paraguay's perspective on the project. In addition, I made a short trip to Asunción where I visited EBY's headquarters in Paraguay, talked to Paraguayan officials, and researched the archives of a local museum that had material on Yacyretá. Undoubtedly this book reflects the fact that research was almost completely carried out in Argentina. But, besides the limitations related to the practicalities of field research, this fact is consistent with the hegemonic role played by Argentina within the project.

Because I was trying to construct a holistic approach to Yacyretá, I also needed to consider broader historical, political, economic, and sociological contexts. At this level of analysis, my objective was to assemble a data base that would allow me to understand questions such as the relationships of the Argentine state primarily and then the Paraguayan state to the Yacyretá project, the political economy of the Argentine energy sector, Yacyretá's politico-economic history, the location of a binational project such as Yacyretá within the framework of the disputes among the La Plata River basin countries, and the importance of the project for regional and national development. To develop a broader vision of my research subject, in Buenos Aires I interviewed high-level Argentine officials directly linked to Argentina's energy sector, followed the discussions on this economic sector in the media, interviewed diplomats specialized on the La Plata River basin, and read published material on Argentina's geopolitical perspective on this South American area. I attended seminars where energy specialists discussed related subjects and did research on material published either by national or international agencies involved with energy production or by specialized Argentine and international periodicals. In the construction of my evidences, I always tried to replicate, whenever possible, information found in one type of source with information found in another type of source.

A final word should be said on my criteria for selecting informants. I selected key informants by considering the amount of power of intervention they had on the project's affairs *and* the amount of power of intervention the project had over them. For that matter, I tried to cover the complete range of individuals who were direct participants in the project, albeit in different positions. Although many of the interviews were carried out in a style that approximates participant observation, doing research in highly hierarchized and institutionalized environments, such as a powerful public corporation, implies a significant exposure to public relations departments and, more importantly, to formal ethnographic encounters where informants were aware of their power positions.

# 2 The Yacyretá Hydroelectric High Dam

A look at Argentina's main sources of energy production reveals an apparent contradiction. Argentina's largest energy resource is its hydroelectric potential, but its principal source of energy has been petroleum. An explanation for this may lie in geographical reasons, such as the long distance between the country's most important consuming centers and the hydroelectric resources, as well as in the political and economic history of the different power groups within the Argentine energy sector.

In spite of the influence of the oil and nuclear lobbies (Da Rosa 1983, 104), in the last two or three decades the Argentine state has promoted the planning and construction of several hydroelectric facilities, including the country's four largest: (1) El Chocón, a 1,200-megawatt (MW) dam completed in 1972 on the Limay River, at the border between the provinces of Neuquén and Río Negro; (2) Piedra del Aguila, a 1,400-MW project constructed on the same river and provincial border; (3) Salto Grande, a 1,900-MW binational project with Uruguay, completed in 1979, on the Uruguay River; and (4) Yacyretá Hydroelectric High Dam, binational with Paraguay, the largest project ever undertaken by Argentina, being constructed on the Paraná River.

The Paraná is the most important of the rivers making up the Río de la Plata basin. It is one of the largest rivers in the world because of its flow, its 3 million square kilometer drainage basin, and its length of about 4,300 kilometers. The Paraná River flows from its source in Brazil into the Río de la Plata, the estuary between Argentina and Uruguay formed by the Paraná and Uruguay rivers (see fig. 1). Oceangoing ships reach as far as Santa Fé, some 600 kilometers from Buenos Aires. The Paraná crosses some of the richest areas of Brazil and Argentina. Along parts of its length it forms the international boundaries between Brazil and Paraguay, and between Argentina and Paraguay.

The Paraná has a great historical, economic, and political importance for a vast area of South America. Since colonial times it has been a most important entryway to the hinterland. It was a seldom used alternative to link the rich Potosí mines region of Bolívia to Spain. Until the 1960s when an international bridge over the Paraná was built linking Paraguayan markets to the Brazilian Atlantic coast, it was the only access that land-locked Paraguay had to world markets.

The Paraná River basin has one of the largest hydroelectric potentials in the world, at present developed mostly by Brazil. Major dams such as Itaipú (12,600 megawatts), a joint Brazilian-Paraguayan project, are either in operation or are planned so as to tap this potential. Da Rosa (1983, 78) lists twenty-five major hydroelectric plants planned or operating on the Río de la Plata basin. The only dam outside the Paraná River basin that Da Rosa mentions is the Salto Grande Argentine-Uruguayan project on the Uruguay River. Garabí is another binational hydroproject, this time an Argentine-Brazilian one, also planned to be built on the Uruguay river. It is a likely result of the regional integration of the Southern Cone, a project that has been led by the Brazilian-Argentine governments since 1986. Of the twenty-five dams listed by Da Rosa, twenty are within Brazilian territory; one (Paraná Médio) is within Argentina; two (Corpus and Yacyretá) are Argentine-Paraguayan projects; one Itaipú, is a Brazilian-Paraguayan work; and the remaining one, Salto Grande, is an Argentine-Uruguayan dam.

The Yacyretá Hydroelectric High Dam is being built on the Paraná River 1,470 kilometers upriver from Buenos Aires to exploit the potential of the Apipé Rapids. The dam site lies on the stretch that separates Argentina and Paraguay, near the Argentine town of Ituzaingó, province of Corrientes, and the Paraguayan town of Ayolas, department of Misiones. Yacyretá is about 100 kilometers downstream from the city of Posadas, which has 140,000 inhabitants and is the capital of the Argentine province of

Misiones, and the city of Encarnación, which has 30,000 inhabitants and is the capital of the Paraguayan department of Itapúa. Forty thousand inhabitants of these cities are going to be affected by the flooding of an area of 1,700 square kilometers, representing the largest number of people estimated to be resettled by Yacyretá's reservoir (Bartolomé 1984). The formation of the new lake will require the relocation of infrastructure works such as railways, ports, highways, sanitation works, and electric and telephone installations.

The work site area of Yacyretá—a binational territory regulated by special laws—covers 1,200 hectares. The infrastructure of the project was completed before the start of the main civil works in December 1983. The work site area includes several villages and encampments, approximately 100 kilometers of access roads in both countries, a 1,500-meter-long bridge over the Añá-Cuá branch of the Paraná River that links Yacyretá Island to Paraguay's mainland. Another 980-meter-long bridge was later constructed over the Principal branch of the Paraná River, linking the island, which is Paraguayan, to Argentina.

Yacyretá's main objective is to provide base-load hydroelectric energy for Argentina's power sector. The dam is also presented as a *multipurpose* project, a term used to qualify several projects. Highlighting secondary benefits and underreporting costs is a common strategy of the promoters of large-scale projects. Thus, besides its power generation objective, Yacyretá is meant to have developmental impact upon navigation by eliminating the rapids of Apipé and by the construction of navigation locks. It is also meant to have positive impacts on irrigation agriculture, flood control, recreation, tourism, fishing, land transport (an international highway passing over the dam is going to link Paraguay and Argentina), and regional development in general.

Whatever the results of the multipurpose scheme, the name Yacyretá will always be associated with energy production. Yacyretá was ranked in 1987 as the world's fourteenth largest capacity hydroplant (Mermel 1987, 43). It is planned to have a final generating capacity of 4,140 megawatts to be accomplished in two stages. The first stage includes twenty turbines with a total capacity of 2,760 megawatts. In the second stage ten additional units will be installed. The first twenty Kaplan turbines, with a rated output of 138 megawatts each, will be assembled and erected in a powerhouse 1,196 meters long and 77 meters wide contructed on Yacyretá Island. Skeleton intakes will be left to receive the ten units of stage two. A reregulating dam is also planned for second-stage construction, located approximately 90 kilometers downstream from the site where the main facilities are being built. If this reregulating dam is constructed, it would add 330 to 620 megawatts of capacity, depending on its location.

Yacyretá Island, with an area of 450 square kilometers, divides the river into two main channels, the Añá-Cuá and Principal branches, on which two closure dams and spillways, with sixteen and eighteen gates, respectively, are under construction (see fig. 2). Besides the powerhouse and the spillways, another important concrete work in Yacyretá is its navigation lock, constructed on the Rincón de Santa María site (Argentine territory). It has a width of 27 meters and a length of 270 meters and will allow the passage of ships with a maximum draft of 3.65 meters, and the lifting of a six-barge tow as much as 23.5 meters in approximately fifteen minutes. It will be the first lock to operate on the Paraná River.

If it is true that there is a world of dam builders, in it Yacyretá is known more for the length of its earth dam than for its works in concrete. Unlike Itaipú, the huge Brazilian-Paraguayan dam built upstream and where the Paraná River runs through a canyon, at the site of the Yacyretá dam the terrain is flat and the Paraná is very broad with characteristics of a lowland river. Thus the Yacyretá embankment acquires exceptional proportions. Therefore, despite the scale of its concrete structures—some 3.1 million cubic meters of concrete will be used in the project—the distinctiveness of Yacyretá lies in its total length of 72.5 kilometers, almost 75 percent within Paraguayan territory. This feature translates into a multitude of technical and production implications that in turn affect the structure of the labor force. For example, earth movement for the construction of this lengthy dike is a central component of the project, indicating the need for a great quantity of off-road trucks, some with a total weight of 92 tons when hauling the maximum 55-ton load, which need to be driven by skilled workers. Not surprisingly, the most powerful section of the construction workers' union at Yacyretá is composed of earth movement workers.

The estimated total costs of Yacyretá have varied significantly. From 1971 to 1987, different sources quote amounts ranging from U.S.$750 million, the estimated cost when the bid for the feasibility study was announced, to U.S.$10.7 billion. Figure 3 illustrates the variation of the estimates over time.

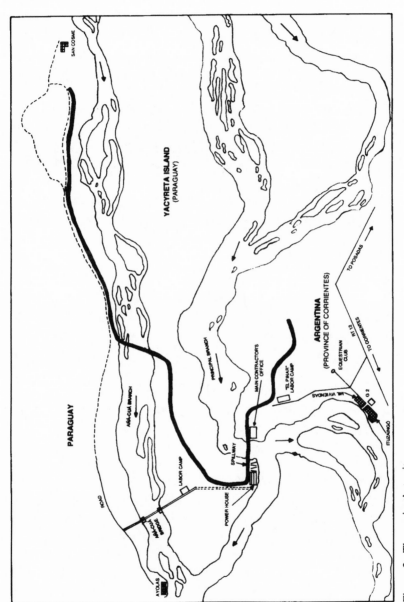

Figure 2. The project's territory

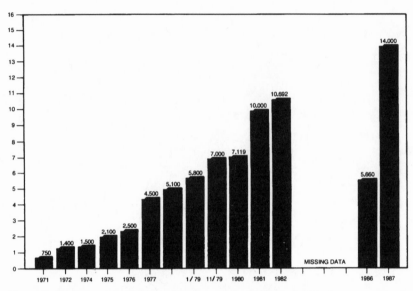

Figure 3. Variations in estimates of total costs (in millions of dollars)

The impressive fall in 1986 is due to a rescheduling of the work, done in 1985, that reduced the total cost of the project by lessening the maximum of the labor force from 9,000 to 6,000 workers thus extending the work over time. In 1987, the expected total period of construction was twelve years instead of the ten years previously planned. The final shape of the graph in figure 3 changes radically if the U.S.$14 billion estimated total cost divulged in 1987 in Buenos Aires is anywhere near correct. After the 1985 rescheduling, 1992 became the deadline for the operations of the first turbines to start. But new reschedulings and delays have occurred since then.

My main sources for elaborating this introduction to some outstanding characteristics of the Yacyretá Hydroelectric High Dam were EBY (1978–81, 1983–84), Harza News (1980), and Revista Construcciones (1985). The civil engineering and electromechanical features of a hydroproject are set forth in a set of complex studies prepared by different specialists—professionals linked to the water and energy development industry—such as civil and electric engineers and geologists. It is self-evident that my aim was not to reproduce this kind of description. From the point of view of a researcher in the social sciences, technical studies are the source of descriptive information, guidelines that allow a plan to become reality. They are seen as blueprints that are marked by an established capability for knowing and solving problems; that is, technical studies are social products relative to a certain historical time and with its possibilities for interpreting and changing natural and social realities.

Actually a project is always an approximation. Its full technical determination is practically impossible to delimit because several features of a work are subject to change as a result of unforeseen physical characteristics of the terrain that may alter the requirements of the foundations or because of natural disasters or economic, social, and political factors that interfere in the scheduling or design of the work. Yacyretá is a case in point. Dam alignment was a major political issue between Paraguay and Argentina because of differential flooded areas in each country. Yacyretá's final design is as much a result of political dynamics as of technical considerations. In this sense, an engineering structure reflects not only technical knowledge as an abstraction but also, and more importantly, the particular combination of people and institutions that are responsible for its elaboration and development. In order to appreciate this aspect of the planning, I now turn to the institutional characteristics of Yacyretá.

### Owner, Consultant, Main Contractor: The Institutional Triangle

The most common model for the development of large-scale projects is based on an institutional triangle composed of the owner, the consultant firm, and the main contractor.

The *owner* is most often a public corporation. It leads the project in its preliminary phases because it organizes the competitive bids through which the other members of the institutional triangle are selected. The owner also promotes the technical and financial arrangements necessary to start both infrastructure and main civil works. Since the owner is responsible for the institutional relationships with other state organisms, and for the future operation of the facilities, it is the most visible public face of a project.

The *consultant* is most often a consortium of several national and international engineering firms. It is usually responsible for the technical guidelines of the project from the feasibility studies through the final plan and design of the work. The consultant is selected in international competitive biddings. It is a powerful actor not only because of its planning, supervising, and monitoring functions, but also because it is highly influential, with technical advice in the process of selecting the main contractor. Despite its power, the consultant occupies the most discreet position within the institutional triangle. This situation is assured by the relatively small size of the consultant's organizational structure compared to that of the owner and main contractor, and by the related facts that it does not have either the public political accountability typical of the owner's position or the large number of employees of the main contractor. On the contrary, in institutional terms, the consultant is characterized mainly by exclusive technical objectives requiring a staff of highly trained personnel. For these reasons, the consultant tends to be the least visible of the three main entities participating in a project.

The *main contractor* is often a consortium of national and international construction firms responsible for the execution of the works. The contract for the main civil engineering work is usually the largest within a project and is awarded through international competitive bidding. The main contractor tends to become the most important actor once the construction of the works starts because, in its executive role, it controls the intricacies of the production process. For this reason, it develops a great amount of minutely detailed knowledge on the characteristics of the work. This creates an asymmetry of information possessed by each member of the project's institutional structure. Consequently, the public corporation (the owner) moves from the leading position in the first stage of a project's organization to a more vulnerable situation. In fact, during the construction of the main civil works, the state has the ownership of the project but does not really control the process. Given the extensive labor force needed to develop a large-scale project, the main contractor is also the main employer of both skilled and unskilled workers. The main contractor's public visibility is also determined by the impressive quantities of resources it manages and by the labor conflicts that unfold during the construction period.

These are the basic characteristics of what I call the institutional triangle. This triangular structure is visible down to the level of the working place, in the simultaneous presence of the main contractor executing the work, of representatives of the consultant supervising the execution of tasks, and of agents of the owner checking and controlling the operation of the system.

## The Owner: The Entidad Binacional Yacyretá (EBY)

Yacyretá, like most large-scale projects, has its own prehistory, that is, a set of previous studies or statements on the importance of accomplishing the construction work. Indeed, the idea of constructing a dam on the site where it is currently being built was formulated in 1920 when the Argentine port authority commissioned a study that included an assessment of the hydroelectric potential of the Apipé Rapids. In 1928 and 1954 other studies were carried out corroborating this assessment.

In the first stages of the Yacyretá project, when the political decision of building the dam had not yet been reached, the main step was the creation of a binational organism in 1958 by the Argentine and Paraguayan states called the Comisión Mixta Técnica Paraguayo-Argentina (CMT), the Mixed Technical Paraguayan-Argentine Commission, the embryo of a future powerful corporation. The CMT was formally established in Buenos Aires on November 3, 1960. It was chartered to promote technical and financial studies and to articulate the complex political and administrative processes that resulted in the creation of the public corporation responsible for the development of the works.

The signing of the Treaty of Yacyretá on December 3, 1973, by the Argentine and Paraguayan governments, marked the culmination of the processes of lobbying and bureaucratic organization that intensified during the last years of the 1960s. The treaty represents the legal instrument formalizing the intention of the two countries to build the dam. It created the Entidad Binacional Yacyretá (EBY), the Yacyretá Binational Entity, that was given the "juridical, financial and administrative capacity, and also technical responsibility to study, project, manage and execute the works . . . to operate and exploit them as a unit from the technical and economic point of view" (EBY 1986, 5). Besides co-ownership of facilities, the Yacyretá Treaty stipulated equal rights to the energy generated by the dam, and a preferential purchasing right over the surplus energy not used by either of the two countries (EBY 1986, 9). The treaty also defined in its Article XI that as much as possible and within comparable conditions, skilled and unskilled manpower, equipment, material, and services should be used in equal proportions from both countries.

The EBY was formally established on September 6, 1974, with head-quarters in Buenos Aires and Asunción, and with a capital of U.S.$100 million equally shared between Agua y Energía Eléctrica (AyEE), the Argentine power authority, and Administración Nacional de Electrici-dad (ANDE), Paraguay's power authority. Besides its Buenos Aires and Asunción's offices, EBY has one office in Posadas (province of Misiones, Argentina) and another in Encarnación (department of Itapúa, Paraguay). These regional headquarters are responsible for the reset-tlement of the population to be affected by the future reservoir. EBY also has field offices in the permanent villages constructed on both sides of the work site in the Argentine town of Ituzaingó and the Paraguayan town of Ayolas. The number of personnel at EBY has increased over the years as follows:

| Year | Paraguayan Personnel | Argentine Personnel | Total |
| --- | --- | --- | --- |
| 1978 | 239 | 211 | 450 |
| 1979 | 293 | 296 | 589 |
| 1983 | 352 | 345 | 697 |
| 1984 | 363 | 472 | 835 |
| 1987 (Feb.) | 495 | 554 | 1,049 |

The statutes of EBY, an annex to the treaty, specified that the members of the board of directors and the executive committee, the highest decision-making bodies within EBY's organization chart, should be appointed half by the Argentine government and half by the Paraguayan one. The statutes also established an "alternate principle" (EBY 1986, 19) within the EBY's power structure, in accordance with which the executive committee positions occupied by Argentine officials for one period should be exer-cised by Paraguayans in the subsequent mandate and vice versa. However, in a side letter signed simultaneously with the treaty (EBY 1986, 67–69), Argentina and Paraguay agreed that during the first two five-year periods (i.e., until September 6, 1984) the strategic positions on the executive committee, namely the executive, technical, and financial directors, would be appointed by Argentina and the legal, administrative, and coordination directors by Paraguay.

In fact, Argentina is the country that has led the project. The Argentine state has historically been the main promoter of the idea and necessity of building the Yacyretá Dam. Paraguay's share of EBY's capital, for instance, was provided by an Argentine loan of U.S.$50 million to the Paraguayan power authority (EBY 1986, 7). It is also the Argentine government that finances the costs of the project with internal and external funds, the largest financing ever developed by Argentina. In the mid-eighties, Yacyretá consumed more than 50 percent of the investments made in public works in this country, a considerable burden for a heavily indebted state especially in times of recession. International loans are exclusively guaranteed by the Argentine government. Once power is generated, Paraguay—which is entitled to 50 percent of total power generation—will pay its share of the investment by selling energy to Argentina.

The significance for Argentina of keeping a leading position in the project's daily management was clear in an administrative reform carried out in 1982. Under Argentine initiative, both the Argentine and Paraguayan governments agreed on December 2, 1982, that the executive director's term scheduled to begin on September 6, 1984, would be defined once more by the Argentine government (EBY 1986, 151). In reality, Argentine officials will occupy the position of executive director, EBY's highest office, for at least three consecutive five-year periods. The administrative reform was also meant to rationalize EBY's bureaucratic and managerial organization, specifically by reducing from twelve to two the number of members of the executive committee, thus facilitating the decision-making process by concentrating power in the figure of the executive director.

In 1987, the internal administrative structure of the binational entity was marked by the six governments Argentina went through since the entity's formal establishment in September 1974 (see table 1). From the Peronist government of María Estela Martínez de Perón (July 1, 1974–March 24, 1976) to the four generals that headed the military juntas of the dictatorship of March 1976 to December 1983, and, finally, to the Radical Party administration of Raúl Alfonsín, which took office on December 10, 1983, the EBY was managed by eight different executive directors. Each of them represented different connections within the various sectors that struggled for power during this period. The result was a layered structure within the Argentine administrative composition of the EBY that was formed by several waves of officials and employees who occupied the institution's top positions and were linked to each succeeding power group.

**Table 2–1.** Argentine Presidents from the 1955 Military Coup to Raúl Alfonsín

| President | Period Served |
| --- | --- |
| Gen. Eduardo A. Lonardi | September 20–November 13, 1955 |
| Gen. Pedro E. Aramburu | November 13, 1955–May 1, 1958 |
| Pres. Arturo Frondizi | May 1, 1958–March 29, 1962 |
| Pres. José María Guido | March 29, 1962–October 12, 1963 |
| Pres. Arturo Umberto Illia | October 12, 1963–June 28, 1966 |
| Gen. Juan Carlos Onganía | June 28, 1966–June 8, 1970 |
| Military Junta | June 8–18, 1970 |
| Gen. Roberto Marcelo Levingston | June 18, 1970–March 23, 1971 |
| Gen. Alejandro Agustín Lanusse | March 23, 1971–May 25, 1973 |
| Pres. Héctor José Cámpora | May 25–July 13, 1973 |
| Pres. (Provisional) Raúl Alberto Lastiri | July 13–October 12, 1973 |
| Pres. Juan Domingo Perón | October 12, 1973–July 1, 1974 |
| Pres. María Estela Martínez de Perón | July 1, 1974–March 24, 1976 |
| Military Junta | March 24–29, 1976 |
| Gen. Jorge Rafael Videla | March 29, 1976–March 29, 1981 |
| Gen. Roberto Viola | March 29–December 21, 1981 |
| Gen. Leopoldo Fortunato Galtieri | December 21, 1981–June 1982 |
| Gen. Reynaldo Bignone | June 1982–December 10, 1983 |
| Pres. Raúl Alfonsín | December 10, 1983–July 8, 1989 |

During the new constitutional government inaugurated in 1983, the relationship between politics and EBY's administration became explicit. A veteran member of the nation's ruling Radical Party, a lawyer and politician from the province of Corrientes, was nominated to the position of executive director. This move was intended both to politicize a supposedly purely technical-economic structure and to respond to Corrientes' (the province where Yacyretá is being built) longstanding claims against the centralization of the project's affairs in Buenos Aires. Indeed, centralism is a historical issue in Argentina. Buenos Aires is a clear example of a primate city that dominates a vast national space (on the formation of the Argentine economic space see Rofman and Romero 1973).

In the process of regionalizing and politicizing EBY's power structure several correntinos and members of the Radical Party were incorporated into the Argentine staff in different positions. *Correntinizar* became a fashionable word. Despite the fact that the elite of the province of Corrientes was guaranteed unprecedented influence over the Yacyretá project, the effort to promote regional participation and development proved to be fruitless. There were two main reasons for the failed attempt: the regional elite's clientelistic conceptions of the management of the immediate benefits of the project, such as job distribution, and the regional elite's inability to deal with an enterprise that is basically oriented by the interests of national and international power groups. Being powerful in Corrientes is not the same as being powerful in Buenos Aires, especially when the scenario of the power struggle is heavily fetichized by discourses based on engineering and financial technicalities.

The retreat was foreseeable: the establishment of another "technical" administration in June 1985. A new executive director, an engineer averse to public notoriety, grounded the project again in the cold foundations of technocratic reason. Yacyretá demonstrated once more that the preferential image of a hydroelectric project is one depicting it as a purely "technical affair."

## The Consultant: Harza y Consorciados, Consultores Internacionales de Yacyretá (CIDY)

The prefeasibility study of Yacyretá was prepared by the Mixed Technical Paraguayan-Argentine Commission (CMT) and was completed in 1964. In 1969, after a period without any major initiatives, West Germany made a loan of DM12 million to the Argentine government for the development of studies related to the Yacyretá project by German and Argentine consultants (*El Clarín*, November 10, 1969). In 1971, the CMT called an international competitive bidding to select a consultant firm to prepare a feasibility study. There were speculations in the Argentine press as to whether national participation would be effective within the would-be consultant and whether Paraguay was as interested in Yacyretá in as much as its partnership with Brazil in the Itaipú binational hydroelectric project, then also in its negotiating stages (*El Clarín*, January 20, 1971).

The request for proposals for a complete technical and economic feasibility study specified that the proponents should be independent consultants from the United States, Canada, Western Europe, and Japan, in each case to be associated with one or more independent Paraguayan or Argentine consultants who should participate to the extent of no less than 50 percent. Selection of the consultant would be made on the basis of qualifications, not on price. Five consortia presented themselves. Besides the mandatory Paraguayan and Argentine partners, there were firms from Germany, Sweden, Great Britain, Switzerland, Italy, United States and Canada (*El Clarín,* June 16, 1971). On August 31, 1971, the CMT announced the winner of the U.S.$4.785 million contract, Harza and Asociados, an international consortium of consultants, formed by Harza Engineering (the lead firm, from Chicago, United States), Lahmeyer International GmbH (Frankfurt, West Germany), Análisis y Desarrollo Económico S.A. (Buenos Aires, Argentina), Yacyretá S.A. (Asunción, Paraguay), and Cuyum S.A.T.C. (Buenos Aires, Argentina). A fifteen-month term was established for completion of the feasibility study. The contract was signed in Asunción on October 20, 1971, in the presence of Argentine and Paraguayan authorities.

The preparation of the feasibility study represented a significant step toward the signing of the Yacyretá Treaty. The study was formally completed in December 1973, the same month the treaty was signed. Among other things, the study defined, at the feasibility level, the dam's alignment, a major issue between the two countries because of the greater amount of Paraguayan territory to be flooded by the reservoir.

In 1973, the CMT called another international competitive bidding to select the consultant for the preparation of the final design and for the technical supervision of the project's execution. Four international consortia, including Harza and Associates, entered the competition. This time, however, the bidding procedures of this multimillion-dollar contract were surrounded by a controversy on the fairness of the selection. In contrast to the first awarding of the feasibility study that was done during the military government of General Alejandro Lanusse (March 23, 1971–May 25, 1973), this bidding process was carried out under civilian rule, and its final stages were defined under the constitutional presidency of Juan Domingo Perón (October 12, 1973–July 1, 1974). Argentine congressmen and the press echoed charges that the selection was going to be decided under the pressures of a pro-Harza Paraguayan lobby, despite the fact that the feasibility study had not proved to be totally satisfactory for the CMT (*El Clarín,* June 9, 1974; *La Nación,* June 13, 1974; *La Razón,* June 23, 1974; *La Prensa,* June 25, 1974). The impasse was due to the fact that Harza did not win the highest score in this bidding process. During June 1974, the CMT held several meetings to solve the question. On June 17, 1974, the CMT decided that Harza, Lahmeyer, and Associates were going to be hired again as consultants.

Most of the final design for the project was done during the period 1974–78. The consultant also designed the infrastructure works related to the relocation plan. Harza y Consorciados, Consultores Internacionales de Yacyretá (CIDY), the consultant's new name, is a consortium formed by Harza, the U.S. lead firm, Lahmeyer, the German partner, COADY, a group of six Argentine engineering firms, and ETIC, a group of six Paraguayan engineering firms. CIDY has a total of four offices, distributed in Asunción and Buenos Aires (the two main design offices), and on the Paraguayan and Argentine sides of the dam's work site (field offices). In June 1984, CIDY had a staff of 333 persons, 107 in Asunción, 151 in Buenos Aires, and 75 at the work site. Almost 36 percent of the total number were professionals (CIDY 1984).

The 1974 decision to continue with the services of Harza proved to be a continuing issue related to the interactions of the several interest and power groups that were articulated within and around the Yacyretá project. In the first months of 1975, during the government of María Estela Martínez de Perón, the question of the fairness of the bidding process was reopened by an Argentine congressman, a member of the Radical Party, who questioned whether the Argentine authorities had acted in the country's best interests (*El Día*, La Plata, February 2, 1975). Later, in October 1980, during the Argentine military regime of March 24, 1976, to December 10, 1983, an ultranationalist vice admiral, who was a representative of a conservative right-wing sector of the Argentine Armed Forces and former vice president during two military governments in the 1950s, declared that the awarding of the consultancy contract was a "transaction between Harza-Lahmeyer and General Alfredo Stroessner," Paraguay's president from 1954 to 1989. These declarations caused considerable diplomatic malaise between Argentina and Paraguay. The vice admiral was arrested for his statements (*ABC-Color,* Asunción, October 9 and 10, 1980; *El Litoral,* Corrientes, November 26, 1980). After the inauguration of the new constitutional Argentine government on December 10, 1983, the Peronist opposition would recall the "doubtful circumstances of the hiring of the consultant" (*Tiempo Argentino,* Buenos Aires, January 27, 1984).

In fact, since its first 1971 contract, the consultant firm has been the center of several allegations, most of them related to its relationships with different segments of the political and economic power system in both countries. As a consequence of its international composition and geographical distribution, the consultant operates in a context in which it manipulates and responds to pressures from the Argentine and Paraguayan states, private construction companies of these countries, and others interested in the construction project. Perhaps the clearest example of such a situation was the long and contradictory process of selection of the main contractor in the early eighties. The Asunción office of CIDY had positions closer to Paraguay's interests. The opposite was true for its Argentine office. In 1986, when the consultancy contract was being renegotiated, one sector of the Peronist opposition questioned the relationships between a powerful member of the ruling Radical Party and the highest decision-making levels of Harza and Associates. The contract for CIDY was renewed in 1986 for U.S.$132 million, for a period ending in December 1996.

Given that CIDY is led by a U.S. firm and, secondarily, by a German one, a significant part of the dam's project was designed outside of Argentina and Paraguay. The fact that the main guidelines for the planning were defined abroad, or by foreign firms that dominate the engineering process, is an indication of the nonlocal or extraregional nature of the project that is clearly perceived by local and regional actors who frequently refer to this situation. At the same time, foreign professionals, hired by the U.S. and German partners of CIDY's consortium, hold important management positions within CIDY's hierarchical structure. They receive higher wages defined at the level of the international market. In Argentina, where engineering is a long-established profession, foreign participation is viewed in terms of the economic and technological dependency it implies. After December 1983, with the new constitutional government, the foreign contribution has declined, supposedly due to a relative increase in power on the part of the Argentine professionals.

## The Main Contractor: ERIDAY–UTE

On September 15, 1983, after what is likely to be one of the longest and most complicated examples of bidding processes, the EBY announced the awarding of a U.S.$1.4 billion main civil works contract to a consortium called ERIDAY–UTE (Empresas Reunidas Impregilo-Dumez y Asociados para Yacyretá–Unión Transitoria de Empresas, United Enterprises Impregilo-Dumez and Associated for Yacyretá–Transitory Union of Enterprises). From the notice of a preselection of proposals that was to be made during 1977's first semester (*El Constructor,* Buenos Aires, December 20, 1976) to the actual award, the bidding process of this contract took almost seven years. It was a highly aggressive competition—with mutual accusations of incompetence and corruption between the two final bidders for the so-called YC-1 billionaire contract.

The consortium that won the contract was actually the fusion of the last competing bidders, two consortia, one led by the Italian firm Impregilo S.p.A. (Milan), an association of three Italian contractors specialized in the construction of large-scale projects outside of Italy, and the other led by Dumez S.A. (Nanterre), a French firm interested in entering Argentina's large-scale project's market traditionally dominated by Italian capital. Impregilo and Dumez accelerated their fusion to facilitate the awarding of the YC-1, since Argentine internal and external politics were rapidly changing as a consequence of the military defeat in the Malvinas War against Great Britain (April 2–June 14, 1982). The post-Malvinas presidency of General Bignone was clearly a transition toward a democratic government. The lobbies with which both Impregilo and Dumez were connected would certainly suffer with the deterioration of the military regime. Furthermore, a boycott that the European Community had held against Argentina because of the Malvinas War also preoccupied Impregilo and Dumez. In Argentina sentiments against awarding the country's largest work to companies whose home countries had supported Great Britain in the international scene were rife.

The ad hoc consortium for Yacyretá, ERIDAY was the legal solution that satisfied the following groups: the thirty-two contractors that it comprised, the World Bank and the Inter-American Development Bank that were supervising the bidding process since they had committed U.S.$210 million each for Yacyretá's construction, and the numerous interest groups that were articulated either within and around the consultant (CIDY) or EBY, both in Paraguay and in Argentina. The seven years of the bidding process of the YC-1 contract took place within the duration of the last Argentine military dictatorship. In consequence, the bid reflects the different contradictions of this period. EBY's decision to award the contract was undoubtedly made considering the imminence of the new constitutional government. It was formalized less than two months before the election of the new civilian rulers.

ERIDAY is a complex combination of international and national capital represented by thirty-two contractors divided into a group composed of thirteen firms led by Impregilo and another group of nineteen associates led by Dumez. Besides the Italian Impregilo that leads the consortium as a whole, and the French Dumez, the co-leader, it includes four other Italian firms, two German ones, one Uruguayan, ten Paraguayan, and thirteen Argentine. It has offices in Buenos Aires, Asunción, and on Yacyretá's work site. ERIDAY's internal power structure is a function of each company's share of the consortium. Impregilo nominates the general manager and Dumez the vice general manager. There are two sub managers, one nominated by the Argentine firms and the other by the Paraguayan group, completing the board of directors.

In February 1986, ERIDAY's European personnel, who were primarily managers and technicians, were composed of the following nationalities: 87 Italians, 47 French, 10 Germans, 3 Austrians, and 1 Spanish, a total of 148 persons, the great majority (94 percent) working at the dam's site. In January 1987, there were 129 Europeans, representing 2.3 percent of ERIDAY's total labor force of 5,627 persons. Despite the contractual formalization of its overall power structure, ERIDAY's daily decision making is often complicated by the clash of Italian and French managerial and technical conceptions. Italian and French managers perceive each other in terms of their ethnic identities and their different previous experiences with other large-scale projects.

The most sensitive issue during the final stages of the negotiations for the establishment of ERIDAY was the percentage of each company's participation, especially those of the Paraguayan and Argentine. Negotiations were held by the consortia led by Impregilo and Dumez. From the beginning, Impregilo's position was that it would not accept a solution that did not include its leadership of the new consortium (*El Cronista Comercial,* Buenos Aires, August 5, 1982). The idea was that the consortia led by Dumez and Impregilo would share the contract in equal parts, keeping their internal divisions. The Paraguayan firms argued that their share of the consortium should be 25 percent rather than the 15.25 percent that was being discussed. Despite arguments on the risks for "national sovereignty" that a smaller share would imply, Paraguayans accepted the 15.25

percent participation in the new society and the offer to construct 12 to 14 percent of the main civil works. Argentina accepted its 34.75 percent share in the consortium without discussion, but argued for the construction of 24 percent of the civil works instead of the proposed 12 percent (*Hoy,* Asunción, February 10, 1983). The final ratios of the Argentine and Paraguayan participations were not officially revealed, but they are supposed to be either the same or close to those mentioned above. Apparently, as part of these negotiations, Impregilo and Dumez also increased Paraguay and Argentina's participations in the main civil works by hiring their Paraguayan and Argentine partners as subcontractors (*ABC-Color,* Asunción, February 19, 1983; *La Prensa,* Buenos Aires, February 22, 1983).

National Paraguayan and Argentine participation has been a permanent issue within the Yacyretá project. It is especially evident in the daily management of the civil works because ERIDAY, a European-controlled consortium, is the most powerful of the actors operating in the construction area. The struggle for defining each company's ratio within the consortium is an example of the negotiations into which national and international corporations entered to defend their interests. A thorough understanding of the national-international composition of ERIDAY should include the evident participation of Italian capital (some of it related to Impregilo) within some of the Argentine companies that are members of Yacyretá's main contractor. Moreover, soon after the constitution of ERIDAY, the Paraguayan Construction Chamber denounced the possibility that a Paraguayan consortium associated with the Dumez group was going to sell a substantial part of its participation to an Italian firm associated with Impregilo's group. Apparently, the negotiations were not completed (*Hoy,* Asunción, April 8 and 15, 1984). For the Paraguayan Construction Chamber, though, it was an indication of the existence in Paraguay of pseudo-construction firms that would participate in the bids only to meet formally the legal conditions related to national capital participation.

## The Meanings of Binationality

The politico-administrative reality of the Yacyretá project must be understood in light of the power relations between the Argentine and Paraguayan states that, in turn, are inserted within the larger context of the international relationships in this region of South America.

Since colonial times, Paraguay and Argentina have a history in many ways related to the Río de la Plata and its tributaries, the Paraná and Paraguay rivers, that were a natural entrance for the Spaniards into the South American hinterland. Control of the Río de la Plata was historically exercised by Buenos Aires. Landlocked Paraguay depended exclusively on this route to trade with world markets until the 1960s, when the growth of Brazil's southeastern economy with its land transportation system created an alternative that linked Paraguay, via Brazilian harbors, to nations other than its neighbors.

Paraguay, Argentina, and Brazil have a long history of triangular relationships. The last two countries are the largest South American powers and have exerted their hegemony to place Paraguay under their political and economic influence with more or less intensity. In the 1960s and 1970s, regional hegemony was a main issue between the governments of Argentina and Brazil, and the Río de la Plata basin its scenario (Da Rosa 1983; see also Betiol 1983, 13–42). Brazil had built several hydroelectric dams in the Paraná River basin and was in the process of beginning the construction of Itaipú, the world's largest capacity hydroplant (12,600 megawatts), with Paraguay.

Following frontier incidents in 1965, caused by a controversy over boundary limits, Brazil and Paraguay signed an agreement in 1966 on the common exploitation of the Paraná River waters. This document is considered the precursor of the Itaipú Treaty (Betiol 1983, 18). Indeed, the disputed area between the two countries was to be flooded by the construction of Itaipú. The fact that the Brazilian-Paraguayan agreement did not include consultations with the downstream countries (Uruguay and especially Argentina) on the use of the international waters of the Paraná, caused considerable malaise. Consequently, the decision to construct Itaipú resulted in a significant deterioration of Argentine-Brazilian relationships. In this context, the possibility of building a third binational project, Corpus, was brought into play. This is another Argentine-Paraguayan hydroelectric plant the site of which lies on a stretch of the Paraná River between Yacyretá and Itaipú, creating hydrologic interdependency between these three dams. Whether Corpus is going to be constructed or not is at present a matter of controversy in Argentina. However, Corpus strengthened Argentina's position. The interdependency between Itaipú and Corpus in terms of the maximization of the use of the river potential, led to negotiations that resulted in a trilateral agreement, the Accord Itaipú-Corpus, signed on October 19, 1979, through which the major issues related to the international status of the Paraná River were resolved (Da Rosa 1983, 95–96).

The Itaipú Treaty was signed on April 26, 1973, providing the basis for the text of the Yacyretá Treaty, signed less than eight months later (Betiol 1983, 27). In fact, one high-level official of the Argentine energy sector, a specialist in Yacyretá, stated that the Treaty of Yacyretá is a translation to the Spanish of the Treaty of Itaipú.

The decision to construct the Yacyretá Dam is intimately related to a geopolitical analysis of Brazil's influence over Paraguay and Argentina's northeast (especially the provinces of Misiones and Corrientes). Geopolitical interpretations are rather diffused in Argentina conforming to an ideology cherished especially by military governments and some nationalist political sectors (for a typical example of an ultranationalist interpretation, see Rojas et al. 1980). On the other hand, the perception of Brazil as an imperialist state is not uncommon in Spanish-speaking South America. There are at least four main reasons to sustain this vision. One is that the common Spanish-colonial past shared by these countries imply a Spanish-centered historical point of view. Brazil's expansion is often interpreted from the direspectful Portuguese that crossed the lines of the Tordesilhas Treaty that in 1494 divided what should be the Spanish and Portuguese empires in the New World. The second reason is that in the past Brazil has incorporated areas of neighboring countries. The clearest example is the purchase from Bolívia of what today is Brazil's Acre State. The third point is that the dynamics of Brazil's economic frontier pressure the neighboring areas of countries such as Paraguay, Argentina, and Bolívia. Finally, a fourth reason is the ideology of some Brazilian military and political sectors of transforming this country into a world superpower.

Yacyretá was a "geopolitical response" to the growth of Brazil's influence and to what was considered Brazilian control over the Paraná River, which increased considerably with Itaipú. In addition to more classical discourses legitimating large-scale projects, anchored either in such technocratic arguments as that Yacyretá was the "least cost solution" for Argentina's energy needs, or in developmentalist conceptions that fostered the idea that the hydroelectric dam would promote socioeconomic growth, the Argentine state legitimated the work taking into account its "geopolitical importance." A statement synthesizing geopolitical arguments offered by various sources might run as follows:

> Making an abstraction of the different political frontiers of the Río de la
> Plata basin countries (Argentina, Bolívia, Brazil, Paraguay, and Uruguay)
> it will be seen that everything disappears but two important economic
> axes, those of Rio–São Paulo and Buenos Aires–Rosário. Bolívia and
> Uruguay are too peripheral to the system, but the same is not true of
> Paraguay, the battleground where the hegemonic destiny of the region
> will be decided until the mid-twenty-first century. The hydroelectric
> works are bridgeheads of this battle that will define the use of this region's
> rich resources. The energy they will produce is a secondary fact when
> their geopolitical importance is considered. Brazil has begun this process.
> Argentina has to match it if it wants to expand its economy and not
> become a Brazilian satellite. The natural and historical area for this
> confrontation is the Paraguayan territory.

This is a well-known model within the Yacyretá project, classified by many as pure "right-wing or military madness." Currently, this line of thought is politically outmoded given the Argentine-Brazilian project of binational integration aimed at the formation of a regional common market that started formally in 1986 during the new civilian regimes. Nonetheless, the bearers and promoters of this model argue that it is the main reason why the Argentine state never abandoned the Yacyretá project, even though it was ruled by different regimes and beset by different problems. Indeed, the negotiator for Argentina of the 1979 Accord Itaipú-Corpus, and Minister of Foreign Relations during General Viola's presidency (March–December 1981) declared:

> The Argentine decision to sign the Yacyretá Treaty aimed at matching
> the Brazilian-Paraguayan achievement, the signing, some months before,
> of the Itaipú Treaty. There was an urgent reason to conclude with
> Paraguay a negotiation that was taking too long and that from the
> geopolitical and geoeconomic point of view could not be postponed . . .
> Yacyretá and Corpus were conceived like development poles. They are
> works that have a geopolitical justification, not only in terms of binational
> relationships, but also in terms of the situation of the Argentine northeast
> as a whole that is submitted to the geoeconomic attraction of the main

Brazilian development pole, this country's southern and central region. This makes it mandatory for Argentina and Paraguay to place in these areas equilibrium points, because good relationships with neighbors are always based upon good relationships of forces. In this connection, Yacyretá represents one necessity for the Argentine northeast and a demonstration that Argentina has the conditions to do jointly with Paraguay great works to equal the attraction that Itaipú exerts. If Argentina did not have the capacity or could not make Yacyretá in the future, its relationships with Paraguay—from now on—would be permanently under criticism. (*ABC-Color,* Asunción, September 26, 1982)

In fact, specialists within the Argentine energy sector and within EBY itself agree that the dam project is uneconomic and that ultimately the reasons for building the dam are the Argentine-Brazilian competition for regional hegemony and the related need to respond to the Brazilian-Paraguayan Itaipú binational project.

Despite the so-called pendular diplomacy that Paraguay practices to defend its interests vis-à-vis Argentina and Brazil, it can be considered a junior partner in both binational projects on the Paraná River (for a discussion on these questions, see Da Rosa 1983). This does not mean, though, that Paraguay has no negotiating power in these processes. The history of Yacyretá shows that, at times, there were central issues for the project's development that were defined by Paraguay's perspective.

Argentina's institutional life was characterized by instability since the creation of the CMT in 1958 until December 1983 (in this period this nation was ruled by fifteen presidents and two military juntas; see table 1). In Paraguay a personalized dictatorship, disguised by the functioning of some Republican institutions such as a closely controlled national congress, was in power from 1954 to 1989. The Argentine-Paraguayan partnership in Yacyretá has been the motive for mutual distrust between the two states which have often raised doubts of each others' willingness to accomplish the project. Since the beginning of the negotiations that led to the 1973 Yacyretá Treaty, Argentina has claimed that its partner was more interested in Itaipú, a project larger than Yacyretá, that was constructed between 1975 and 1982. Itaipú caused a developmental wave in Paraguay who participated in the project with half of a 40,000-man work force. Itaipú's total cost was estimated to be U.S.$15 billion, of which U.S.$1 billion was transferred to Paraguay during the construction period (*La Voz,* Córdoba, April 13, 1983).

Being the third part of the triangle that defines the core of the Río de la Plata basin's regional problems gave to the elite of Paraguay, one of the poorest countries in South America, the possibility of planning its future in terms of becoming an energy-exporting nation. Yacyretá was seen not only as a way of compensating for the end of Itaipú's developmental wave, but also as an assurance that "electrodollars" were the basis on which Paraguay's future could be planned. In this sense, Yacyretá had a different importance for each country involved in it. For Argentina it represented the most important project the country was willing to develop to reaffirm its presence as a major state in the region. For Paraguay it signified an experience—subordinated to Itaipú's previous one—that would further and consolidate a new and powerful connection of its national economy, which is marked by contraband and corruption, with the international market. From this position, Paraguay gained time and accumulated knowledge from the Itaipú process to negotiate its new commitments.

Yacyretá's binationality caused several issues between Argentina and Paraguay. Some issues were related to the inclusion of Paraguayan capital in the largest contracts of the work, such as the main civil works and turbine contracts. Others were related to the amount of materials made in Paraguay to be used in the dam's construction. The quantity of cement is a typical example. Argentina also protested the financial amount estimated for the land slated to be flooded in the Paraguayan territory. The argument was that areas owned by high-level Paraguayan authorities were over-priced. Of all the controversial points, two proved to be the most difficult to resolve: the rate of exchange issue and the dam alignment that involved compensation for flooded territory.

Since Argentina is the country that finances the project, the payment for Paraguayan services and materials is calculated in guaraní, Paraguay's currency, converted to U.S. dollars, and transferred from Buenos Aires to Asunción. The Paraguayan government has kept the guaraní overvalued so that for the same amount of guaranís more U.S. dollars have to be transferred by the Argentine government. On several occasions Argentina stopped or severely diminished the flow of dollars to Paraguay, causing an indebtedness of the EBY office in Asunción. For instance, during most of 1982 Argentina was transferring approximately U.S.$1 million a month to

EBY-Asunción (*Hoy,* Asunción, November 15, 1982); Paraguayan firms that were owed several million dollars pressured their government. Argentina claimed that Paraguay should have a "realistic" guaraní exchange rate because the difference between the official rate and the free market rate was significant. Argentina proposed a parity of 160 guaraníes/U.S. dollar, while Paraguay defended the 126 guaraníes official rate (*Hoy,* Asunción, December 19, 1982). Paraguay also claimed that the country's monetary policy was a question of sovereignty and could not be negotiated under pressure from a foreign state. The impasse lasted several months. In August 1983, the difference between the official Paraguayan rate and Asunción's free market rate was 160 percent (*El Cronista Comercial,* Buenos Aires, August 4, 1983). Finally, the solution came with the establishment of a guaraní/U.S. dollar parity at an intermediary value between the official and Asunción's free market rates.

During repeated negotiations over the years, Paraguay often questioned whether Argentina was really interested in constructing Yacyretá (see, for instance, *ABC-Color,* Asunción, August 21, 1983). Later, in October 1985, the exchange rate would become an important issue again. Argentina was transferring dollars using a 240 guaraníes/U.S. dollar rate, while in Paraguay the free market rate was 775 guaraníes/U.S. dollar. Again, Argentines wanted to establish a "more realistic" rate. The flow of capital from Buenos Aires to Asunción stopped. Consequently, Paraguay stopped the works in its territory where more than 70 percent of the activity is carried out, to pressure Argentina to restart the flow of U.S. dollars (*Ambito Financiero,* Buenos Aires, October 8, 1985). The guaraní rate of exchange is a question that has remained a potential source of conflict (see *La Razón,* Buenos Aires, January 3, 1986).

These were not the only times that one of the two countries threatened to definitely halt the project. Perhaps the most critical issue in this direction was the definition of the dam alignment, a conflict that unfolded at different times. Indeed, the definition of the dam alignment was the first main controversy between Argentina and Paraguay. The issue was first raised in 1972 during the preparation of the feasibility studies when several designs, with various technical and financial implications, were proposed. Argentina favored a less expensive solution that would imply a larger amount of flooded Paraguayan territory (*La Razón,* Buenos Aires, August 5, 1972). Paraguay chose a more expensive design that would preserve a larger amount of Paraguayan territory (*ABC-Color,* Asunción, August 8, 1972). The proposal was immediately interpreted in Argentina as a sub-mission of the Paraguayan government to Brazilian interests related to the binational hydroelectric project of Itaipú (*El Cronista Comercial,* Buenos Aires, August 16, 1972). The Paraguayan-Argentine relationships entered a cold and tense period that coincided with the transition from General Lanusse's dictatorship (March 23, 1971–May 25, 1973) to the beginning of Juan Domingo Perón's presidency (October 12, 1973–July 1, 1974). In the interim Argentina had two presidents, in preparation for Perón's return to power (for a description of this period see Maceyra 1986). During the presidency of Perón, who maintained a long-standing relationship with Paraguay's dictator, General Stroessner, a definition of the dam alignment was reached at the feasibility studies level with the aim of signing the Yacyretá Treaty in December 1973.

Nevertheless, the problem was not resolved. It reappeared some years later during the so-called El Proceso, short for Proceso de Reorganización Nacional, the Argentine military dictatorship of March 1976 to December 1983. After what seemed an agreement on the dam's alignment formalized in 1977 with the signing of side letters by the two governments (EBY 1986; 83–84), the issue was reopened in 1979 with great intensity. Mean-while, these negotiations, as well as the delays in the prequalification process of the main contractor, had already caused a general delay of twelve months that meant an increase in the cost of the project of about U.S.$150 million.

Paraguay's argument was that with the dam alignment agreed upon in 1977, its flooded area would be almost five times greater than Argentina's (*Ultima Hora,* Asunción, March 10, 1979), something that a country with territorial scarcity could not support. Argentina denied the possibility of changing the dam's alignment given the technical, financial, and safety problems this would cause the project. The media of the two countries began an information war. The project entered a period of several months of uncertainty, with officials of the two countries constantly traveling the Asunción–Buenos Aires route. The World Bank and Inter-American De-velopment Bank, who had committed themselves to partially finance the works, pressured for a resolution of the impasse: August 31, 1979 was the deadline after which the international loans would be canceled. Stroessner in Paraguay and the ruling military junta headed by Videla in Argentina held several meetings to consider the issue. The possibility of solution came when the discussion turned from the dam's alignment to the establishment of a compensation arrangement for flooded territories. A compromise was reached by a compensation arrangement under which EBY would pay compensation for the flooding of Paraguayan and Argentine territories once the hydroelectric dam was in full operation. The new agreement was formalized with side letters between the two countries signed on August 30, 1979, just one day before the bank deadline. Paraguay and Argentina would receive U.S.$21 million and U.S.$6 million per year respectively (*Mercado,* Buenos Aires, September 6, 1979). This compensation is to be paid by Argentine power consumers as a result of what were obscure negotiations, a common solution in a project with which the word corruption is often associated (years later, Carlos Menem, the Argentine president, called Yacyretá a "well of corruption," *Jornal de Brasília,* April 4, 1990).

Paraguayan authorities denied that they were bargaining for other benefits during the course of the negotiations, such as infrastructure works, benefits that Argentina would commit to build for Paraguay in order to reach a solution. Videla and Stroessner met three times in one month. Their second meeting, on November 6, 1979, was to sign the World Bank and Inter-American Development Bank loans for Yacyretá, in the neighboring cities of Posadas (Argentina) and Encarnación (Paraguay). On November 28 and 29, three months after the end of the dam's alignment issue, the presidents of both countries signed an agreement through which it was determined, that, among other things, to facilitate Paraguay's world trade, this country would have a free zone in the Argentine harbor of Rosário on the Paraná River, and that Argentina would finance the construction of one bridge, two schools, and two roads in Paraguay (*Convicción,* Buenos Aires, November 30, 1979). This document announced that the necessary measures to start the construction of the Posadas-Encarnación bridge over the Paraná River had begun. This is a major bridge of 2.5 kilometers linking the Paraguayan town of Encarnación to the Argentine Posadas, located some 100 kilometers away from Yacyretá's work site. It was later agreed that EBY would finance this "complementary work" (*El Cronista Comercial,* Buenos Aires, July 3, 1981), which was considered to be the main immediate advantage Paraguay obtained in compensation for its flooded territory.

# 3 The Power of a Dam: Articulating Power Groups

Besides extensive amounts of capital and labor, the construction of a hydroelectric dam requires that its leading participants be familiar with complex technological and managerial procedures. The magnitude of the resources needed and the complexity of the arrangements involved in the production process are factors that limit access to the main contracts for large-scale projects to corporations that already operate at national or international levels. In the engineering industry large-scale projects are the cream of the market and contracts are highly contested by the top firms in the sector.

The relationship between large-scale projects and leading consultants and contractors implies a two-way movement. Large-scale projects require large corporations, and large corporations look for opportunities to design and construct large-scale projects and stimulate the market for them by indicating and proposing new works. Corporations also define the effective dimensions of projects by taking into account organizational, technological, and financial constraints.

Other than civil engineering, several industrial branches take an active part in the construction of a hydroelectric dam. The electric and steel industries are important protagonists in the production process: turbines, cranes, generators, and transmission lines, for example, are important components of a hydroelectric project. Large-scale projects are also a market for specialized heavy equipment such as off-road trucks. The complete set of requirements and elements needed for the civil engineering and electromechanical works cannot usually be provided within a single national political entity. There are, for instance, few steel mills capable of producing the impressive turbines needed for a dam as large as Yacyretá. A huge dam is a world market happening that articulates national and international industrial capital with the mediation of national states.

In addition to the technological and managerial complexities created by and for a project, the scale of required financing makes it necessary to look for credit from different international sources. Indeed, the capital needed to develop a large-scale project almost always amounts to several billion dollars. There is no single source that would commit itself to financing the totality of a large-scale project. Consequently, financial capital also becomes associated with such a project in an intricate way. The financial package is a composition of international, national, private, and public capital most of the time guaranteed or supervised by the project owner's government, multilateral agencies, and regional development banks. Yacyretá, for instance, is financed by the Argentine government electrical funds; the World Bank and Inter-American Development Bank that partially finance the main civil works; Export-Import Banks that finance the bulk of the heavy construction, power generation, and electromechanical equipment; and several international private banks.

The diversity of financial sources in a project underpins the participation of several transnational firms. A common financing mechanism is the so-called export or tied credit, that is, credit that is given to a project's owner in case it purchases services or equipment from the country of the financing source. Most industrialized countries have official banks that subsidize their national exports called Ex-Im Banks. Firms of these countries frequently rely on the lobbying of these powerful agencies and the special loan conditions of the official credit they offer. The description of the bidding process for the turbines contract for Yacyretá will provide examples of these transactions. Clearly, a contractor who participates in a bidding that is backed by special financing has a distinct advantage.

The active participation of Ex-Im Banks in these processes makes clear how major nation-states protect their industrial capital. The U.S. case provides an interesting illustration. Apparently, subsidizing financial capital for major U.S. industrial corporations was a main cause of the U.S.

Ex-Im Bank's growing losses. In 1987, the "financial health" of this official bank was a motif of consideration among the political and business communities of the United States. According to the *New York Times* (December 21, 1987) "behind the red ink are loans made in the late 1970s and early 1980s when interest rates soared. The bank lends to customers of American exporters at rates below the cost of the money it borrows from the Treasury. . . . the difference between the Ex-Im Bank's average cost of its money and what it receives from its loans was still around 3.5 percentage points through most of this year."

The international character of a large-scale project is further reinforced by the presence of multilateral financing agencies, invariable actors of the so-called development projects. The loans these agencies regularly make to hydroelectric projects give them important supervising and guarantor roles such as those performed jointly by the World Bank and the Inter-American Development Bank (IDB) in the Yacyretá project. The connections between multilateral agencies, class-biased development, and the preservation and reproduction of international capital on a world scale is clearly shown in Cheryl Payer's book on the World Bank (Payer 1982, 359–60, for instance).

Among multilateral agencies the pattern of operation of the World Bank is archetypical. Most of its loans and credit are made for specific projects, electric power projects being a traditional World Bank type of lending. For Payer "electrical power projects have been considered particularly suitable for bank lending because they are heavily capital intensive, requiring expensive imported equipment produced mostly by the developed countries. As an 'old-style' bank project, this sector has been vulnerable to the deserved charges that its benefits go only to the already wealthy and powerful" (1982, 100–101). Since 1962, the bank has been involved with the energy sector in Argentina and until the late 1970s made loans to the major utility serving the Buenos Aires region, SEGBA, and for the construction of the 1,200-megawatt El Chocón hydroelectric power plant. Typically, it has pressured the Argentine government to implement a more realistic pricing policy for all energy products.

The World Bank's presence in a project may be relatively less important in monetary terms than in its meaning to other financing sources as a guarantee of appraisal and supervision by an agency that acts like an "organizer of creditors" (Just Faaland quoted by Payer 1982, 17). In

Yacyretá, for instance, when the financial package was being elaborated, a World Bank loan of U.S.$210 million, to be paid over a period of fifteen years including a six-year grace period, was valued more for what it meant in terms of the bank's international power as a guarantee that would facilitate the participation of other sources of capital than for the amount per se (*El Economista,* Buenos Aires, January 19, 1979). This is a strong reason why the promoters of large-scale projects seek this multilateral agency's involvement. World Bank's support or lack of it may seal the fate of a project, because access to international sources of capital can become extremely complicated.

Naturally, beneficiaries of World Bank loans must comply with bank requirements. The power of the World Bank was evident in Yacyretá in moments such as the hiring of the consultant, Harza and Consorciados, Consultores Internacionales de Yacyretá (CIDY), when the contract that formalized the transaction was submitted to the bank and considered satisfactory by it. The awarding of the main civil works contract was also defined when the bank approved it. World Bank power is also felt on a more regular basis because it negotiated standards that Entidad Binacional Yacyretá (EBY) had to follow. These "agreements and recommendations" allowed for substantial influence over EBY as well as over the Argentine energy sector as a whole. These recommendations included items related to the evolution of the organization of the Argentine energy sector, the execution of acceptable environmental and resettlement programs, the financing and accounting system of the project, and the control of EBY's debt, for instance.

The most evident way through which the World Bank ties large-scale projects to the interests of private international capital is by "insisting on procurement through international competitive bidding (ICB), which favors the largest multinationals" (Payer 1982, 19). Most World Bank loans and credit are allocated through ICB and are supervised by the bank. For Payer (1982, 36) ICBs have failed to eliminate abuses in the system; they are ineffective against cartels, such as the ones commonly found in the electrical equipment supply industry; and they are also instrumental in keeping poorer countries dependent upon international capital.

The fact that ICBs make the participation of transnational corporations mandatory for the project owners to have access to international capital is not the only reason they are important. They are also the visible scenario where international and national capitalist firms meet to compete for the award of million-dollar contracts. A large-scale project is a world of joint ventures. In the selection of the winners, the representatives of national ruling elites have a prominent role operating through the public company that owns the project. The state is thus an active and powerful participant since the public corporation is the actor that formally organizes and defines the bidding processes. National and international firms fight for their share, pressuring national governments. The final decision is the result of long, complex, and sometimes harsh power negotiations. Corruption, networking, media blitzes, juridical demands, lobbying abroad and at the project's home country are some examples of the measures taken to win the bidding war.

The intensity of a government's response to the pressures brought by national companies depends on the relative power of the national bourgeoisies to impose their role as an active development actor. In the case of Yacyretá the unequal development of the production forces from Paraguay and Argentina was an important factor in governing the varied articulations of Paraguayan and Argentine elites with the representatives of international capital. These differences in participation, in turn, depend on the relative development of the many industrial branches intervening in a project.

In Argentina, for instance, the cement industry has reached a level of economic and political importance such that Loma Negra, one of the most powerful Argentine corporations, has become almost the exclusive supplier of cement to Yacyretá, displacing and subordinating the interests of Paraguay who did not possess a cement industry as strong as Argentina's. The Argentine steel industry was also powerful enough to secure for itself a substantial participation in the making of the turbines for Yacyretá. The argument of national companies is that their positions within a project must be assured in the name of policies supposed to stimulate national development.

Given the state's importance in the process, political networks are an outstanding consideration for both national and international participants. Inclusion in a country's political life is, then, a cherished and valuable asset. Both national and international firms are aware of this and identify their associates not only by technical and financial characteristics, but also by their political connections and capacities.

Briefly, ICBs are crucial for the understanding of the dynamics of a hydroelectric dam such as Yacyretá because they are the scenario where international and national capital become entangled, clearly introducing political and power contexts. The state plays an important role by setting the stage and acting as referee, supervised by mighty multilateral agencies. The competition begins when the other actors, the transnational and national corporations, encounter and make use of all their available means to win the contracts.

## Significant Examples of Bidding Processes within the Yacyretá Project

The procession of numerous power groups through the Argentine state marks the history of the Yacyretá project and is a most important factor complicating the bidding processes of the project's largest contracts. The succession of high-level officials meant different conceptions of national energy policy with varying emphasis or interpretations on the role of thermal and hydroplants in power generation. As a consequence, the interplay of lobby groups defending the interests of national and international capital with the representatives of the Argentine state is a central characteristic that needs to be considered. The state, or rather its surrogate, the public company, may be seen as a field of tensions, as the locus where the conflicting and contradictory articulations of national and international interests occur.

Yacyretá's largest contracts are those related to the main civil works and the turbines, the so-called YC-1 and YE-1(t) contracts. Among several other contracts, those corresponding to the provision of generators, main transformers, powerhouse cranes, spillways and powerhouse locks, and equipment for the navigation locks stand out. The procurement of these contracts is typically made through ICB. The bids for the infrastructure works, preliminary tasks such as the construction of transportation and communication systems, and for permanent camps in the Argentine town of Ituzaingó and in the Paraguayan town of Ayolas were awarded with the exclusive participation of national companies. The same is true for the works associated with the resettlement of the population to be affected by the reservoir.

The established rules of the bidding processes create similar formalities among them. Their differences relate to the particular industrial branches that they refer to (engineering, metallurgy, electric) and their varying relative development and power connections within Argentina and Paraguay.

The complexities of the two largest contracts, YC-1 and YE-1(t), provide the best scenario to scrutinize the equation formed by the state and the transnational and national corporations. The description and understanding of these bidding processes are necessary before getting to the discussion of a process I call *consortiation*. A detailed consideration of the awarding of the main civil works contract, YC-1, will be followed by a more succinct description of the turbines contract, YE-1(t), because most of the conjunctural factors are considered while analyzing the YC-1 case. My intention in presenting the YE-1(t) case is to provide a comparative frame that allows me to highlight the greater negotiating power of the Argentine metallurgic industry in relationship to transnational corporations and the state, as well as a different financing scheme, and the subordination of Paraguay to the clear position of junior partner.

Despite the fact that the turbines contract was awarded in 1987 during the new Argentine civilian government, its fate was basically defined during the four governments of the military dictatorship of March 1976–December 1983, the so-called El Proceso, (short for the "Process of National Reorganization"). The main civil works contract, the most important one since the dam is above all a construction work, was defined during the Proceso. A brief characterization of the 1976–83 military regime is needed in order to understand the wider context in which these bidding processes unfolded.

### An Approximation of El Proceso, Argentina's Military Dictatorship (March 1976–December 1983)

Although the relationships of power groups during the military regime of 1976–83 were generally subordinated to the attempt to adjust Argentina to a "new international division of labor, modernizing its structures in function of the interests of transnational capital, monopolistic national sectors and financial capital" (Paz 1985, 88), they were neither homogeneous nor harmonious. This would become evident after the end of General Jorge Videla's government in March 1981 when the mighty economics minister left the power scene, fragmenting the coalitions and alliances that maintained Videla during five years as the head of the ruling military junta.

The direct or indirect support of private international banks and multilateral agencies for the military coup and regime is asserted by some authors (Paz 1985, 89; Vitale 1986, 283–90, for instance). There is little reason to doubt that those who controlled international capital felt more comfortable with the predictability of the alliances they could develop under the military regime than with the economic and political instability of the last years of the María Estela Martínez de Perón government. International bankers gave more than U.S.$1 billion in credit to Argentina during Videla's first two years of government (Conklin and Davidson 1986, 237–38). The International Monetary Fund (IMF) signed a standby agreement in August 1976, three months after the coup. In an article on the history of the involvement of the IMF in the Argentine economy, Conklin and Davidson concluded that from 1958 to 1985, this fund's "stabilization programs" besides being unsatisfactory from an economic, social, and political point of view have meant "a decrease in the standard of living for a significant portion of the population" and have "been linked to the forceful repression of labor and political instability." Moreover, far from promoting development, IMF's presence in Argentina has "contributed to violations of the economic and social human rights" of Argentine citizens (Conklin and Davidson 1986, 262).

World Bank relationships with Argentina after the 1976 military coup also increased rapidly. The negotiations for a major amount of credit for the construction of Yacyretá were accelerated under the initiative of the new economics minister who, in a meeting of the IMF in the Philippines, declared that the World Bank and the Inter-American Development Bank were considering a joint financing of Yacyretá (*La Opinión*, Buenos Aires, October 10, 1976). In August 1977 the subsecretary of Hydroelectric and Thermal Energy announced that both banks had "given the green light" to the financing of Yacyretá (*El Territorio*, Posadas, August 28, 1977).

The displacement of national capital by international capital, especially capital in the manufacturing industry, was consistent with a process of deindustrialization that was fed by an economic policy that opened up Argentina's domestic market and overvalued the Argentine peso. The result was the closure of a large number of nationally owned industries that could not compete with the waves of imported products. The financial policy of the period is registered in Argentines' memory as the *plata dulce* time, literally "sweet bucks" time. From 1976 to 1983 the foreign debt increased from U.S.$8.3 billion to U.S.$44.5 billion (Vitale 1986, 286). According to Pedro Paz (1985, 97), U.S.$23.4 billion, that is, almost two-thirds of the U.S.$35.6 billion Argentine debt as of December 1981, was literally stolen in a "financial orgy." *Patria financiera,* financial homeland, was the label Argentines coined to represent the hegemony of financial capital.

The energy sector was a favorite masking device for the entry of external funds that would never be applied to the production process. Years later, in 1986, the president of the Argentine Water and Power authority (AyE) regretted the financial state of his company that had on June 30 of the same year a foreign debt of U.S.$2.07 billion, "70 percent of which does not correspond to investments something that is equivalent to admit that, like in other public corporations of the energy sector, AyE was one of the windows used to give entrance to foreign funds and maintain the foreign exchange policy followed during the military regime" (*Informador Industrial,* no. 90, July 1986).

Massive evasion of hard currencies, financial speculation, a fall of real wages, the concentration of capital, together with the exponential growth of the foreign debt and the partial liquidation of the national industry were the main economic effects of the Proceso's developmental policy. The economic program of the dictatorship represented an attempt to restructure Argentine social organization by changing class relationships and favoring a process of concentrating capital, in contrast to previous developmentalist trends based on import substitution, in turn more connected with distributivist conceptions (see Azpiazu et al. 1986, 89, 122–24, 185–203). This program's political implications were the most severe in Argentina's contemporary history. The national congress was closed. Censorship and intolerance were the daily rules. Political adversaries were persecuted and disappeared. Conklin and Davidson (1986, 238–39) quote figures as high as 5,000 arrests during the first four months of Videla's government and Amnesty International estimated that 15,000 people "disappeared." The working class was the main target of state terrorism. According to Conklin and Davidson, an official investigative commission found that "workers accounted for 30.2 percent of the disappearances—more than any other sector of the society."

Totalitarian power was not enough for the groups struggling within the military dictatorship. Despite amassing one of the most impressive concentrations of power a Latin American regime has had, an internecine power struggle began to develop after Videla's five-year period of rule. General Roberto Viola's government began in March 1981. It was held in a contradictory grid of interests and was heir to an economic plan that was reaching its political limits. The Viola period is characterized by overall administrative indecision. As a consequence of the power void and internal conflicts in the military, General Leopoldo Galtieri overthrew General Viola in December 1981. The decline of the military dictatorship was under way. With the defeat in the Malvinas War (April 1982–June 1982) against Great Britain, the military forced Galtieri out of office and began a period of transition that was to end in December 1983 with a new democratic government.

Before the new constitutional government of December 1983, the military intended to close the Proceso period and negotiate some of its pending questions. The endless dance of economic and political power groups around the Yacyretá project was one of the main scandals of the military dictatorship. In August 1982, General Reynaldo Bignone, the head of the last military junta (June 1982–December 1983), appointed a new executive director for the EBY. The executive director's task was to finalize the awarding of the main civil works contract (YC-1) before the inauguration of the next constitutional government. On September 15, 1983, forty-five days before national elections of the new constitutional authorities, the YC-1 contract was awarded. The goal was reached; Yacyretá became an irreversible reality. Although some arguments were presented for political and juridical revisions of the project contract, the main political parties that would once more rule Argentina assumed the responsibility for the country's "work of the century."

## The Bidding Process of the Main Civil Works Contract (YC-1)

The YC-1 contract is the largest within the Yacyretá project. Since the first rumors in the last months of 1975 that the YC-1 bidding process was about to begin, the structuring of behind-the-scene connections formed part of the history of this contract. There were suspicions concerning linkages of powerful officials with the consultant aimed at influencing the consultant's prominent role in the contract's award decision (*Prensa Confidencial,* October 8, 1975). In December 1976, news in an Argentine civil engineering publication announced a public and international preselection of proposals (*El Constructor,* December 20, 1976). Apparently this prequalification was never carried out. Videla's government decided to begin new studies, causing considerable delay for the project. This decision was made in a context where lobbies linked to the interests of thermal plants were highly influential. The first executive director (September 1974–November 1976) for EBY would later state that he was fired by Videla's mighty economics minister as a way of protracting the execution of the project. According to him the "pro-thermal" energy interests first formed by British coal-fired thermal plants would progressively become associated with local interests: "they are not many, but are individuals that exert a lot of power because of the positions they occupy. They get connected with all de facto governments, and from within them impulse their plans" (*ABC-Color,* Asunción, September 15, 1982). The assertions of a former financial director and an ex-juridical consultant confirmed the influence of the pro-thermal lobby in the first moments of Videla's government (*ABC-Color,* Asunción, September 11, 17, 18, 1982).

In February 1978, another competition for the YC-1 was announced. The importance and repercussion of the U.S.$1.4 billion main civil works contract attracted the attention of eighty-five contractors from seventeen countries organized in fifteen consortia. Twenty-two of these eighty-five companies were from Argentina, fourteen from Paraguay, ten from Italy, six from Mexico, five from Korea, five from West Germany, four from Spain, four from Holland, three from Brazil, three from France, two from the United States, two from Yugoslavia, and the five remaining from Switzerland, Sweden, Uruguay, Canada, and Taiwan (see EBY 1978, 16–17).

In 1979 many steps were taken toward making Yacyretá a reality: several bids were announced; the Accord Itaipú-Corpus disentangled the Argentine-Paraguayan-Brazilian impasse over the international use of the Paraná River; the dam alignment issue, a factor of tension between Argentina and Paraguay, was resolved; and, in October, five consortia previously prequalified received the bidding conditions for the main civil works contract. Besides Empresa Constructora Yacyretá led by Impregilo and the consortium led by Dumez, the other preselected consortia were: Yacyretá Joint Venture, led by Dragados y Construcciones S.A., Spain; ICA S.A. and Associates, led by Ingenieros Civiles Asociados S.A., Mexico; and Morrison-Knudsen International Company Inc., United States

(EBY 1979, 20). The bidding established that the consortia should be led by foreign companies to "avoid rivalry between the sister Republics of Paraguay and Argentina" (Botana 1982, 39). On June 2, 1980, the five contenders presented their offers priced as follows:

| | |
|---|---|
| Dumez Consortium | U.S.$1.480 billion |
| Impregilo | U.S.$1.706 billion |
| Dragados | U.S.$1.764 billion |
| ICA | U.S.$1.811 billion |
| Morrison-Knudsen | U.S.$2.390 billion |

With the advice of CIDY, its consultant, EBY had only a few months to study the offers and indicate the winner of the contract. This was the beginning of a long process in which the number of likely awardees was reduced to two: the consortium led by the French contractor, Dumez, and that led by Italian Impregilo. Dumez's strongest card was that it offered the cheapest proposal. In the competition for a contract, bidders always try to offer the lowest bid because price is a financial and politically decisive criterion. The guidelines for procurement of the World Bank, the ultimate referee of the YC-1 contract award, moreover, favor the awarding to the bidder with the least expensive offer. But Impregilo's strongest asset was that in Argentina, where Italian capital became a predominant factor in the engineering industry after World War II (Panaia 1985, 23), the company had been in the center of the country's hydroprojects construction market since the 1960s.

The first moments of the tug-of-war between the two top contenders for the YC-1 contract witnessed a lobbying visit of a Dumez mission to Buenos Aires and Asunción at the end of August 1980, with an immediate demand by Impregilo that Dumez be rejected on the basis that it had not complied with the bidding conditions (*La Razón*, August 22, 1980; *ABC-Color*, Asunción, August 26–28, 1980). Impregilo's main arguments during the almost three-and-a-half-year period of the contest were that Dumez (1) had deliberately omitted a price-adjustment formula, (2) did not present either an adequate method for closing the cofferdam or an adequate timetable, (3) did not foresee the construction either of a service bridge linking Argentina with Yacyretá Island (Paraguay) or of temporary camps, and (4) was trying to manipulate labor costs by establishing low wages, excluding workers' meals from its calculations, and by proposing the possibility of importing cheap foreign labor (see, for instance, *ABC-Color,* May 4, 1981, that published a letter in which Impregilo lists its objections). The last considerations were important because Impregilo could insist that their competitor's inexperience in Argentina implied a misconception of local labor relations that would lead to a management of the labor force doomed to constant confrontations with the Argentine unions and, consequently, to cost overruns. Impregilo was evidently maximizing its social and political capital in Argentina. It had built or was building the largest Argentine hydroprojects such as El Chocón, Planicie Banderita, Alicurá, and Salto Grande, and it was in a position to transfer to Yacyretá the equipment, labor force, and experience it had accumulated working under Argentine conditions. Furthermore, their Paraguayan partner in the bidding was CONEMPA, a consortium that participated in the construction of Itaipú, that had a large labor force experienced in another huge binational hydroproject to contribute to Yacyretá.

Despite the efforts made by Dumez in Argentina, Paraguay was undoubtedly its main ally; strong lobbying could be more effective in a country in which the large-scale project market was not dominated by its contender. Binationality was manipulated by the two competing consortia: the consultant's office in Paraguay tended to back the awarding of the contract to Dumez, while Impregilo was CIDY's choice in Buenos Aires. The consultant's personnel who participated in the study of Dumez and Impregilo's proposals, both in Asunción and Buenos Aires, have not forgotten the political pressures to which they were exposed.

Before reaching to a point where the binationality line clearly split into a Paraguayan/pro-Dumez side versus an Argentine/pro-Impregilo side, the process became complicated by the dynamics of the internal struggles within Argentina's military regime.

*"The competition for Yacyretá is a sort of horse race in which everything is allowed" (Botana 1982, 95).* In the competition for the contract, Dumez, lacking Impregilo's several years in the Argentine market, established a lobby by recruiting influential figures from Buenos Aires's elite. The most tangible evidence of this group's existence and activity is the book *El Caldero de Yacyretá* (Botana 1982). This book is replete with allusions to the Catholic faith. Its last sentence, for instance is in Latin:

*Finito Libro sit Laud Deo Christo et Mariae.* This rare mixture in a pragmatic tool for very mundane objectives must be understood in light of the frequent use of religious discourse, by factions of Argentina's conservative elite, to construct an acceptable and legitimate identity. Argentina is a Catholic country where the church hierarchy is eminently conservative and has played important symbolic and political roles within the country's ruling elite. This is especially true for the period of the military dictatorship that was closely connected with the Catholic church and that subscribed to the most regressive practices of religious intolerance. From a literary and logical point of view *El Caldero de Yacyretá* is a badly written book, with old and inelegant metaphors based on moral, religious, or historical prejudices that are supposed to denote erudition. The author does not hesitate to resort to anecdotes that are intended to expose what he per ceives as his opponents' (i.e., Impregilo's backers) reproachful social and cultural habits. As a piece of the lobbying war, this book is evidently a one-sided perspective. Nevertheless, its importance as a source of information, which I compared with information published in Argentine and Paraguayan newspapers as well as with the interviews I did with Argentine officials, stems exactly from its biased perspective: it was written to debilitate Impregilo's power connections by publicizing them. There are references to industrial espionage, betrayals by people who were working for one side and were bribed by the other, and backstage agreements between the bidders to manipulate the result of the award (see Botana 1982, 43,44,47).

The power of the Italian consortium became clear in the first months of 1981. In January of that year, a report by the consultant (CIDY) that was widely publicized in Paraguay, though less so in Argentina, recommended that EBY start negotiations with Dumez and, if these reached a satisfactory result, to award the main civil works contract to the consortium led by the French company. The central point was the U.S.$226 million difference between Dumez and Impregilo's proposals. The Argentine government, however, faced a conjuncture because of the transition with the approaching inauguration of General Viola's administration in March 1981. There was an overlap between the power groups related to General Videla's departing government and General Viola's incoming administration. This ambiguity was reflected within the EBY. The decision to award the YC-1 contract was subordinated to the expected change of

*Juntas Militares* (*El Territorio,* Posadas, January 30, 1981; *ABC-Color,* Asunción, February 19, 1981).

Following the consultant's indication, EBY's executive director intended to award the contract to Dumez. With the active participation of Impregilo's lobby, the decision was finally postponed. Apparently, the intention was to give General Viola an important task with which to begin his government in March 1981: the awarding of the country's largest public project. In the meantime, the executive director who had been nominated during General Videla's government was experiencing a gradual loss of power within EBY. This corresponded to the increased influence of the financial director, a protégé of the entering president, General Viola (for this period see Botana 1982, 105ff.). Following his progressive isolation within the new power structure that was defining the fate of the YC-1 contract, the executive director resigned on April 21, 1981, less than one month after the inauguration of the Viola government.

The direction of EBY remained uncertain for almost two months, a period in which new factors were produced. The most important one was a report that was attributed to the consultant, fabricating criticisms of the Dumez offer. This document was sent to the highest Argentine authorities, the World Bank, and Inter-American Development Bank, who were all supervising the awarding of the YC-1 contract. This "report" was published and discussed by the Argentine press (*Buenos Aires Herald,* September 10, 1981; Botana 1982, 120–21). The forgery was discovered, causing further conflicts among the directors of EBY. The battle culminated in the firing of one director who had written a report stating that the Dumez offer could not be disqualified under the allegation that it did not comply totally with the bidding conditions because this was also true for the other proposals. He also concluded that the awarding had to take into account the U.S.$226 million difference between the two best offers; otherwise "moral values, like the correct behavior, good name and prestige of the responsible officials would be exposed to doubts and suspicions hard to dissipate" (this report, dated April 6 was published by a Paraguayan newspaper, *La Tribuna,* November 3, 1981).

The next chapter in the struggle for hegemony within Yacyretá centered around the departure of the finance director in September 1981. He had survived various executive directors and was subsecretary of Finances and Foreign Investments of the national government, General Viola's protégé, and, according to Botana (1982, 90), one of the most important allies of the Impregilo lobby. The fact that he was at the same time EBY's financial director and subsecretary of Finances and Foreign Investment of the national government was the immediate reason to force his leave. The underlying factor was that he was considered a competitor of the executive director's power within EBY's hierarchical structure. Indeed, the executive director had to wait for several weeks until the resignation of this financial director.

The overall political uncertainty of General Viola's brief government (March 1981–December 1981) was increasingly felt within Yacyretá. During this period EBY had no clear directives on what decisions to make on the YC-1 contract. The Paraguayan government attributed the project's delay to Argentina (*La Tribuna,* Asunción, August 28, 1981). There was a change of executive directors, and the different lobby groups were restructuring their compositions and strategies. The new executive director held several meetings on the YC-1 contract issue with the Argentine president without coming to a definite official conclusion. The awarding of the YC-1 was one of the most common subjects in the Argentine press.

In August 1981, EBY's new executive director, appointed in June 1981 by Viola, sent his report on the awarding of the YC-1 to the Argentine presidency recommending the contract be awarded to Dumez (Botana 1982, 153). The document was not accepted. The unofficial decision of the Argentine government to award the work to Impregilo was clear.

As part of the lobby war, first Dumez, and later Impregilo, published page-long advertisements in Argentine and Paraguayan newspapers in October and November 1981 defending their offers. The following are some of the Argentine newspapers in which Dumez published its advertisement on October 29, 1981: *La Prensa, El Cronista Comercial, Ambito Financiero, El Clarín, La Nación.* On November 1, 1981, Impregilo matched its opponent by publishing a larger advertisement in those same newspapers plus *Convicción* and *La Razón.* Dumez's message finished by stating that Argentina and Paraguay should not pay a higher price for the Yacyretá project. Its last sentence was a metaphor indicative of the qualities of the power conflicts that had been developing for several months; it was an appeal to "moral values": "What is really at stake is the greatest of all reasons: Justice." Impregilo's pragmatism and self-assurance based on its Argentine networks might be what led the company to begin its advertisement by making allusion to the general difficulties the leadership of El Proceso, the military dictatorship, was confronting. It stated that the company had broken silence with the intention of "avoiding confusions that affect not only Yacyretá but *El Proceso.*" The message's introduction is an attempt to demonstrate an identity between the military dictatorship and the company.

The Paraguayan government, however, did not intend to share a surcharge of U.S.$226 million, especially because this overcost did not have a strong technical justification. The Paraguayan adjunct executive director had declared to an Asunción newspaper (*ABC-Color*) in May 1981 that "Argentina's sympathy with Impregilo was a withdrawal from the established norms" (quoted in *La Nueva Provincia,* Bahía Blanca, November 3, 1981). Argentine authorities tried a final move: to offer Paraguay a compensation in public works to accept the transaction (*Hoy,* Asunción, October 28, 1981; Botana 1982, 150). Meanwhile, CIDY, the consultant, prepared another report, this time recommending that the award go to Impregilo.

Since the bidding process was supervised by the World Bank and the IDB, a mission was sent to Washington to obtain their endorsement. In the first days of November, the executive director of EBY made an "informal" presentation of its conclusions to these banks. At the same time the Paraguayan ambassador in Washington told the press that Impregilo would construct Yacyretá (*Ultima Hora,* Asunción, November 6, 1981; *La Prensa,* Buenos Aires, November 8, 1981). In reality, he was making public a decision that could not be officially confirmed because EBY had to wait for the assessment the World Bank and IDB were to make on the new situation. The decision-making center was now displaced to Washington.

But, Argentine political instability would intervene once more. General Viola was overthrown by the military, and the new Junta Militar began its rule on December 21, 1981. Argentina was heading for even more instability.

The drastic measures on public expenditures announced by General Galtieri, the head of the new junta, affected Yacyretá to such an extent that doubts whether the project would be carried out at all returned to the foreground. The new ruler's connections with thermoelectric lobbies produced additional uncertainty about the project's future. The two first months of 1982 were marked by (a) discussions on the budgetary deficit; (b) what was seen as a misunderstanding by the new Junta Militar of the geopolitical value of Yacyretá ("'Strategic needs are not measured in dollars,'' wrote *Convicción,* a newspaper linked to the Navy, on January 14, 1982); and (c) the expectation on the World Bank's position on the report that the executive directors had taken to Washington in November 1981.

Repeated rumors that the project would be discontinued provoked the mobilization of local populations in the provinces of Corrientes and Misiones. In the Correntina town of Ituzaingó, the people of the area where Yacyretá was going to be constructed demonstrated against the possibility of dismissing the project. The rally was organized by the town's chamber of commerce and industry. The governor of Corrientes, another general, playing the role of his province's spokesman on the Yacyretá issue, asked for an appointment with General Galtieri in Buenos Aires. His appointment with the president—widely publicized as a regional defense of the project—was denied (*La Nación,* March 3, 1982).

In the first days of March 1982, an official of the World Bank visited Buenos Aires, bringing with him the bank's position on EBY's intention of awarding the YC-1 contract to Impregilo. Following the argument that Dumez had presented the least expensive offer, the bank suggested that EBY should enter contractual negotiations with Dumez, but added that it would not have any objection if EBY preferred to make another proposal. The World Bank was immediately classified as pro-Dumez and accused of interfering in Argentina's internal affairs (*La Prensa,* March 6, 1982).

*Convicción,* a newspaper that five days before had defended Yacyretá, agitating the fear of Brazilian influence on Argentina's northeast, published an article on March 7, 1982, with the following heading: ''Are Chileans the ones that do not want us to make Yacyretá?'' Chile is another of Argentina's ''geopolitical concerns.'' During the El Proceso military dictatorship, Argentines almost went to war against Chile because of frontier problems over the Beagle Canal. The common interpretation is that Chile has a permanent goal of incorporating the Patagonia Region into its national territory to have access to harbors on the Atlantic Ocean. The following is a translation of a part of the article published by *Convicción*:

> The World Bank is doing everything it can to delay or to definitively hinder the construction of Yacyretá. Beyond the pressures that Dumez can exert on the World Bank, it is a mistake to believe that this is only a battle between the Dumez and Impregilo corporations. This is what is visible.

What is not that visible is the "coincidence" that it was . . . the Chilean representative at the World Bank who has been placing the largest obstacles for the awarding of the credit to Argentina. And what is more astonishing is that [this official], this Chilean [official] is presently in Buenos Aires, trying to convince the Argentine government that there should be a new bid on Yacyretá. That means to delay the work for five or six years. Better saying, never doing it. It seems that Chile has already "decided" for us.

Concurrently, EBY's executive director resigned on March 25. He had been experiencing a gradual loss of power since General Viola's government and then faced General Galtieri's lack of interest in Yacyretá. During these three months of Galtieri's government the executive director did not receive any orientation on Yacyretá's place within the new government plans. On the contrary, he was "systematically excluded from the committees and meetings carried out to analyze the future of the Entity and the work" (*Hoy,* Asunción, March 27, 1982). Uncertainty ruled at EBY, which was leaderless for several months.

In fact, Argentina was on the eve of an even more unstable political and institutional time. The climax came with the Malvinas War against Great Britain (April 2, 1982–June 14, 1982) when the country entered a period of war effort. Yacyretá was a secondary issue during these months of public commotion in Argentina. The beginning of all new public works was suspended; the priority was defense expenditures (*El Clarín,* April 12, 1982). Meanwhile, the two top contenders for the main civil works contract became increasingly aware of the risk of losing the possibility of constructing the dam. The World Bank had not accepted the report that favored the awarding of the YC-1 to Impregilo, and insisted that negotiations should be carried out with Dumez, the contractor who had presented the lowest bid. Under these circumstances the two consortia began a process of negotiations that would lead to their fusion into a new entity: ERIDAY (see chapter 2).

The Malvinas defeat signaled the end of the military regime and the beginning of a period of transition toward democracy. The perspective of a constitutional civilian government in a post-Malvinas period as well as a growth of nationalist conceptions became a distinct possibility. Both France and Italy were in disfavor with some military factions because as members of the European Community they had supported Great Britain by participating in an economic boycott and voting against Argentina in the United Nations during the war. Furthermore, these countries began to put pressure on the Argentine dictatorship, because the crimes against human rights committed during the military regime began to be discussed openly.

The awarding of YC-1 had to be accelerated and the fusion of the two consortia was a solution. Rumors about the imminent fusion were constantly reported in the press. The military junta that was organizing the transition to democracy, declared, through General Bignone, the last military president, that it favored the concretion of Yacyretá (*El Territorio,* Posadas, June 30, 1982). A new executive director began his mandate on September 1982 with the explicit goal of awarding the YC-1 contract. In November, Argentina's minister of public works announced the fusion of Impregilo and Dumez (*Convicción,* November 12, 1982).

At the same time, an administrative reform of EBY was formalized, simplifying the decision-making process by concentrating power in the executive director. Some days later the World Bank and the IDB approved the fusion of Dumez and Impregilo (*Hoy,* Asunción, December 15, 1982). In the first semester of 1983, the thirty-two contractors led by Impregilo and Dumez negotiated the legal creation of ERIDAY. The frequent exchange of information between EBY and the World Bank is another indication of this institution's prevailing role in the final stages of the awarding of the main civil works contract. Finally, on September 15, 1983, the U.S.$1.4 billion contract was officially awarded to ERIDAY. The signing of the contract between EBY and ERIDAY on October 20 was the last act of what is certainly an example of one of the most complicated bidding processes. On December 3, 1983, ten years after the signing of the Yacyretá Treaty the main civil works were officially started. The new constitutional government that was inaugurated one week later (December 10) had to deal with a de facto situation.

### The Bidding Process of the Turbines: The YE-1(t) Contract

The YE-1 contract represents the electromechanical segment of the Yacyretá project. The YE-1 is a set of multimillion-dollar contracts that, since they were first announced in a prequalification call in 1976, attracted several transnational corporations. The set of twenty 138-megawatt Kaplan-type turbines—the largest in the world with 9.5 meter-diameter each—was the most expensive part of the electromechanical components. The YE-1 contract covers other electromechanical components of the Yacyretá Hydroelectric Dam such as generators and regulators. Not all corporations that participated in the bidding process of the YE-1 contract presented offers to all of its segments. I will consider only the process that led to the awarding of the turbines, the so-called YE-1(t) contract. For simplicity sake, instead of YE-1(t) I will use the term YE-1 to designate the turbines contract.

Some of the largest corporations in the world entered the competition for the turbines segment of the YE-1 contract. In December 1978, EBY preselected seventeen contenders to participate in the YE-1 contract bidding. There were three consortia: ACWEST, formed by Allis-Chalmers Corporation and Westinghouse (United States); Yacyretá-Apipé, formed by Siemens AG (West Germany), Energomachexport (USSR) and G.I.E. (Italy); and Japan Consortium (Mitsubishi, Hitachi, Toshiba, Fuji) and Voith (West Germany). Nine individual firms were also preselected. In addition, five other participants were selected under conditions. These last fourteen corporations were based in France, Yugoslavia, Sweden, England, Austria, Switzerland, Czechoslovakia, Spain, West Germany, Canada, and the United States (see EBY 1978, 19).

The availability of an adequate and attractive financing scheme—the so-called export credits—is a common way of enhancing a corporation's competitiveness in a bidding process. Special financing offered by export-import banks is as important as a corporation's reputation. In this connection, the governments of these corporations' countries back their industries with special credit packages that are going to be open to the purchasing country. Consequently, during decisive moments in the bidding process of the YE-1 contract, pressures from governments favoring their own contenders were intense. Several governments of the competing bidders sent lobbying missions. Until the definition of the top contenders, Argentina and, secondarily, Paraguay were visited by the U.S. subsecretary of Commerce (March 1980), U.S.S.R.'s vice minister of Foreign Trade (April 1980), an Austrian mission (June 1980), and the minister of International Trade of Canada (September 1980). All of them had Yacyretá as a main subject of their agenda.

But, since the first moments of what was going to be another long bidding process (resolved only in 1987), the most important actors were clearly defined. On one side was the American corporation Allis-Chalmers and the U.S. Ex-Im Bank, on the other, METANAC, a consortium of Argentine metallurgic industries.

*The Turbine War.* The massive violations of human rights by the military dictatorship furnished the reason for pressures from the Carter administration on the Argentine government. One of the episodes of this confrontation included in July and August 1978 restrictions on a loan that the U.S. Ex-Im Bank would make available to Allis-Chalmers to compete for the procurement of Yacyretá's turbines (*El Argentino,* Gualeguaychú, July 28, 1978; *La Arena,* Santa Rosa, August 22, 1978). Less than two years later, however, when the project was at a more stable juncture, a U.S. lobbying mission, formed by high-level government officials and managers of the U.S. corporations interested in Yacyretá, visited Buenos Aires and Asunción. The participants of this mission included the U.S. subsecretary of Commerce, one director of the Ex-Im Bank, an adjunct vice secretary of State, the president of Allis-Chalmers's board of directors, the vice president of Westinghouse's board of directors, and the vice president of Morrison-Knudsen company, among others (*El Clarín,* March 10, 1980; *ABC-Color,* Asunción, March 11, 1980). They announced the availability of a U.S.$700 million Ex-Im Bank credit to finance the purchase of U.S. equipment and machinery to Yacyretá, if U.S. corporations won the contract. In an optimistic and positive atmosphere, where General Videla's economic policy was praised, the U.S. vice secretary of Commerce affirmed the Carter administration's "new vision of the commercial relationships with Argentina," and that Ex-Im Bank's loans were independent of human rights or other subjects of international politics. Ex-Im Bank offered a twenty-year loan with a ten-year grace period at an interest rate of 7.75 percent per year (*La Nación,* Buenos Aires, March 12, 1980).

Allis-Chalmers was now in a strong position to compete with the other international corporations and with the representatives of Argentina's heavy industry that claimed a greater national participation. Four months later, in July 1980, with an offer of U.S.$172 million, Allis-Chalmers was considered the strongest candidate for the awarding of the turbines contract. The bids on the turbines were:

| Allis-Chalmers Corp. (United States) | U.S.$172.0 million |
|---|---|
| Dominion Engineering Co. (Canada) | U.S.$182.2 million |
| Consortium Yacyretá-Apipé (Energomachexport, USSR; Siemens, West Germany; GIE, Italy) | U.S.$201.5 million |
| Neyrpic-Voest (France-Austria) | U.S.$201.6 million |
| Mitsubishi & Voith (Japan, West Germany) | U.S.$233.3 million |
| Boving-METANAC (England, Argentina) | U.S.$242.2 million |
| Escher Wyss (Switzerland) | U.S.$305.8 million |

The participation of the Soviet Energomachexport in the Yacyretá-Apipé consortium was controversial in Argentina as well as in Paraguay. The Soviet Union is a traditional purchaser of Argentine grains and beef. The commercial balance between the two countries is historically favorable to Argentina. The purchasing of equipment, especially for the energy sector, is a frequently mentioned way of compensating for this difference (*Convicción*, April 11, 1980). Indeed, the Soviet Union had supplied Argentina with turbines before, for the Salto Grande binational project on the Uruguay River. Their competitors, however, divulged that these turbines were not delivered on schedule, and more importantly, that not all of them were in perfect order. But the most influential argument against Energomachexport's participation was politically grounded. One of the ideological bases of Paraguay's three-decade-old dictatorship was a fierce anticommunism. Paraguay did not have diplomatic relations with the Soviet Union and, despite favorable financial conditions, was radically against the purchasing of turbines from that country. Typical anticommunist rhetoric in relation to the possibility of awarding part of the generators contract to Energomachexport was a common item in the Paraguayan press (*ABC-Color*, Asunción, October 24, 1981, for instance).

The financing scheme of the Soviet partner of the Yacyretá-Apipé consortium had the following characteristics: the period of grace would cover the whole construction period, payments would begin with the dam's completion and operation, and continue over a ten-year period with a 4.5 percent interest rate per year. The Soviet Union would commit herself to purchase from Argentina 70 percent of the value of the YE-1 contract in traditional export goods, and the remaining 30 percent in nontraditional exports. At least one Argentine newspaper published an article stating that the Soviet turbines for Salto Grande had had no problems (*Ámbito Financiero,* January 28, 1981).

Nevertheless, it was clear that Allis-Chalmers was the most powerful contender in what the Argentine press called the turbine war. Its strongest adversary proved to be METANAC, the consortium of Argentine metallurgic industries, associated with the English Boving, the lead firm. METANAC was created in 1978 with the objective of participating in large-scale energy projects in general and in particular, for the bids for Yacyretá's locks and turbines. Four major Argentine corporations associated to form the new consortium: COMETARSA (Construcciones Metálicas Argentinas S.A.), Astilleros Príncipe y Menghi, Establecimientos Industriales FEBO S.A., and especially IMPSA (Industrias Metalúrgicas Pescarmona), all of them with previous experience in Argentine hydroelectric projects. Since its creation METANAC insisted that national participation at Yacyretá depended on political decisions, and that it was important to give the Argentine industry a precedent to enable it to compete in other ICBs of works of the same scale as Yacyretá (*Veritas,* May 15, 1979).

Boving-METANAC bid for ten turbines of which the Argentine consortium would make five. Each METANAC turbine would cost U.S.$600,000 more than those of the cheapest offer. But, asked IMPSA's president, the leading metallurgic corporation in Argentina, "is it worth losing the benefits of producing them in the country because of this difference?" (*El Clarín,* Buenos Aires, December 9, 1980). The most frequent arguments for a strong participation of national industry were that this work would imply a contribution to the development of the country in general because it would represent, for instance, one million hours of Argentine work; it would not be wise strategically to depend solely on one supplier; and the Argentine government's support would be to the benefit of the national state because local producers are also local taxpayers. In order to increase the competitiveness of METANAC it was also suggested that the taxes they would pay in connection with the production of the turbines be reduced.

Allis-Chalmers was aware of the sensitivity of the national participation issue. In fact, since 1978 it had been negotiating the formation of a concern with AFNE (Astilleros y Fábricas Navales del Estado S.A.), Argentina's state-owned shipbuilders controlled by the Navy. AFNE-Allis would be controlled by the U.S. corporation (by ownership of 80 percent of its capital) and would construct a U.S.$40 million plant in case it was awarded the YE-1 contract. In the course of the negotiations Allis-Chalmers offered Argentina a participation of 6 percent, in case they were awarded ten turbines, and 14 percent if they obtained the contract for the full set of twenty. These percentages covered only small parts of the equipment (*El Economista,* November 28, 1980). For Allis-Chalmers, the Yacyretá contract represented a possibility to recover from an increasingly debilitating economic situation.

The Argentine government was considering splitting the contract to different bidders. Nonetheless, Allis-Chalmers had a strong ally: the U.S. Ex-Im Bank and its U.S.$700 million loan. In the beginning of Ronald Reagan's administration, in a visit to Washington, the Argentine and Paraguayan foreign ministers were informed of the U.S. government's interest in the procurement of electromechanical equipment (*Convicción,* Buenos Aires, September 2, 1981; *ABC-Color,* Asunción, September 2, 1981). More importantly, the Argentine minister was reminded that the U.S. Ex-Im Bank had established September 15, 1981, as the deadline after which the U.S.$700 million loan's interest rate would change from a 7.75 percent yearly rate to 10.75 percent.

Under these circumstances, METANAC was offered participation as a subcontractor for AFNE-Allis, Allis-Chalmers's local partner and subcontractor. METANAC's political power was clear. The consortium had entered the competition for the YE-1 contract associated with Boving, but now was a candidate to build turbines under Allis-Chalmers's leadership. This situation prompted another bidder, a Canadian-based corporation, to send a letter to the Junta Militar and to EBY stating that the bidding process of the YE-1 contract "was far from any logic and causality" (*La Nación,* Buenos Aires, September 15, 1981). But Allis-Chalmers's offer was not accepted by METANAC, which had recently won (April 1981) an important contract to make the spillways locks, and aspired to build at least three or four turbines. METANAC insisted that a position like the proposed one did not guarantee the consortium a status that represented the precedent it needed to enable it to participate in other ICBs.

Under pressure of Ex-Im Bank's deadline, on September 11, 1981, EBY declared that Allis-Chalmers was the "most convenient offer," a legal solution that allowed further negotiations with AFNE-Allis and METANAC. In fact, an agreement was reached in November 1981. Under terms of this contract, Allis-Chalmers was to supply sixteen turbines, two of which had to be constructed by AFNE-Allis. The remaining four turbines were contracted for U.S.$24 million to METANAC (*Engineering News Review,* November 15, 1983).

The year of 1982 was marked by the overall deterioration of the Argentine dictatorship accelerated by the military defeat in the Malvinas War. In relationship to Yacyretá the predominant question was the urge for a definition of the main civil works contract. But an important fact related to the YE-1 turbines contract began to unfold in the 1982–83 period: the deterioration of the AFNE-Allis association. Allis-Chalmers was given a term, ending in April 1982, to make the necessary investments to open its new factory with AFNE in Argentina. The deadline had passed and the transition government of General Bignone was not favorable to the concessions of a new period. In this context, Allis-Chalmers considered the dissolution of the partnership with AFNE and a restructuring of its offer. The space was opened for a greater participation of the Argentine private industry that began to postulate the making of ten turbines (*El Cronista Comercial,* March 15 and April 27, 1983). In light of the prospects of more Argentine national participation, the U.S. Ex-Im Bank reduced its loan from U.S.$700 million to U.S.$400 million and called for negotiations on the exceptionally good 7.75 percent yearly interest rate that would be maintained to cover only the turbines but not the heavy machinery imported from the United States (*El Clarín,* April 21 and 24, 1983). In the second semester of 1983 a new accord was reached under which Allis-Chalmers would build twelve turbines with no local participation and METANAC would fabricate the remaining eight with technical assistance from Allis-Chalmers (*Engineering News Review,* November 15, 1983). Paraguay's share would be the mounting of thirteen turbines by CIE, Consorcio de Ingeniería Electromecánica S.A., (*La Nación,* January 15, 1983).

After the inauguration of the new civilian government (December 1983) an increasingly powerful factor came to the fore: Argentina's foreign debt. During a long period Ex-Im Bank's loan to EBY depended on the negotiations the Argentine government carried out with the International Monetary Fund (IMF) and with the international banking members of the Paris Club (*Ultima Hora,* Asunción, June 11, 1984). The dynamics of the international conjuncture had also changed the values of the different currencies of the YE-1 bidders' countries of origin. These movements had made the German and French offers especially attractive (*El Periodista de Buenos Aires,* January 18–24, 1985).

But Allis-Chalmers's financial conditions worsened significantly with the increasing difficulties it was experiencing in its home country and in the world market. In the last months of December 1984 rumors of Allis-Chalmers's bankruptcy were intense in Argentina. They lent fresh support to the argument for greater national participation. The possibility of engaging other international corporations such as Dominion Engineering Works, Canada, began to be considered (*La Prensa,* Buenos Aires, January 11, 1985). In these circumstances the strongest candidate for the awarding of the YE-1 contract would rapidly become a new consortium formed by Allis-Chalmers and Dominion Engineering Works. The latter had offered, years ago, the second lowest bid. At the same time, there were rumors of intentions to start conversations with Voith, another of the original bidders. This German corporation had claimed that by accepting successive requests of reformulations of the original offers, EBY was breaking the principle of equality of treatment that should rule any bidding process (*La Razón,* February 13 and 15, 1985). In view of this situation, Voith GmbH wanted to be considered again as an active competitor for the YE-1 procurement.

On March 14, 1985 EBY announced that its board of directors had approved the awarding of the turbines contract for U.S.$213.8 million to the Allis-Chalmers/Dominion Engineering Work consortium. Legal conditionalities included the presentation by the two firms of a joint guarantee, the implementation of U.S.-Ex-Im Bank's loan of U.S.$400 million (still on hold because of Argentina's foreign debt problems), and the attainment of an export credit from the Export Development Corporation of Canada. Allis-Chalmers would fabricate nine turbines, Dominion Engineering Works, four, and METANAC, seven. Paraguayan firms would participate in the mounting of the equipment. Local supplies would be financed by special credit lines of the Argentine Central Bank (*El Territorio,* Posadas, March 15, 1985). On March 19, Ex-Im Bank and EBY signed a loan agreement for U.S.$400 million. This credit, however, would remain nonoperational for a long period because it continued to be subsumed to the negotiations of the Argentine debt with the IMF and the Paris Club. The YE-1 contract award was not signed.

In 1985 the financial difficulties of Yacyretá caused by a lack of external financing and the overall Argentine economic crisis, led to a rescheduling of the project. The peak of the work force was substantially diminished, postponing the completion date from 1990 to 1992. The problems of the Argentine economy were directly reflected in Yacyretá's main internal source of funds, the Fondo Nacional de Obras Eléctricas (National Fund for Electrical Works). In 1986, for instance, this fund transferred to Yacyretá less than two-thirds of its assigned contribution to the project. Yacyretá had to obtain the difference from the Argentine Treasury or from international creditors. In 1987, the internal financing situation worsened (*El Cronista Comercial,* January 16, 1987). Indeed, during this year, out of an estimated U.S.$200–80 million contribution, nothing came from the National Fund for Electrical Works.

The delays on the signing of the YE-1 contract also meant extra financial costs to the project. Since 1983, when Argentina accepted the U.S. Ex-Im Bank loan, the country had to pay U.S.$2 million annually, a 0.5 percent commitment commission. This loan was unblocked only in January 1987. Increasingly dependent on foreign financing, in December 1986 EBY obtained a loan of U.S.$63 million from the Export Development Corporation of Canada to cover 85 percent of the Canadian imports (*Ultima Hora,* Asunción, December 12, 1986). A new U.S.$900 million World Bank and IDB loan was expected to be received in 1987. This credit was conditioned upon adjustments of the electric tariffs, a classic World Bank condition (*El Clarín,* Buenos Aires, October 25, 1987).

Although the awarding of the YE-1 contract had been approved in March 1985, it was signed only in mid-1987. The main factors preventing a solution were the fact that Allis-Chalmers and Dominion still had not formally concluded the creation of the new consortium, together with the Argentine debt crisis. At the same time, the rumors of Allis-Chalmers's bankruptcy proved to be correct. The conditions of this corporation worsened considerably with its economic deterioration in its home country. Allis-Chalmers's problems had aggravated to a point that its Hydro Division was sold to German Voith GmbH in September 1986 (*Ambito Financiero,* Buenos Aires, August 1, 1986).

On May 22, 1987, EBY's board of directors authorized the signing of the award for the turbines contract for U.S.$270 million. Finally, in the last week of June, in the Paraguayan town of Ayolas, the contract was signed between EBY and the winning consortium. German Voith, that had acquired Allis-Chalmers and continued to benefit from U.S. Ex-Im Bank's loan, would fabricate nine turbines, Canadian Dominion Engineering Works, four turbines, and METANAC, the Argentine heavy-industry consortium, seven. Paraguay's Consorcio de Ingeniería Electromecánica would produce components equivalent to the costs of one turbine (*El Clarín*, Buenos Aires, June 28, 1987). This was the end of a bidding process taking almost eleven years.

## Comparative Comments on the YC-1 and YE-1 Cases

The description of both bidding processes highlights the difficulties of generalizing and finding a common underlying pattern. In Yacyretá this is further complicated by the binational character of the project. Paraguay and Argentina are countries with different levels of development of their production forces. Despite Paraguay's bargaining power, an emphasis on the Argentine characteristics of these processes is appropriate since the hegemony of Argentina is unquestionable.

Although the bidding for the YE-1 contract was subject to the same political instability that caused the frequent changes of EBY's top management, its distinguishing characteristic, in contrast, was the active and almost constant confrontation between Argentine heavy industry and foreign interests, especially those represented by Allis-Chalmers and the Ex-Im Bank. During the bidding process for the main civil works there was not a significant resistance by Argentine contractors to the dominance of foreign companies. Comparatively, Argentine heavy industry counted on greater support from the Argentine state, including during the military dictatorship. The greater sensibility of the Argentine dictatorship to the claims of the steel industry was consistent with the military policy of favoring monopolistic capital. Moreover, it showed that this Argentine industrial sector was more powerful than the construction industry that did not—or could not—pressure the military regime with the same intensity as the steel-making companies did. It must be added that behind the leadership of IMPSA—the largest member of METANAC—there was not only the power of monopolistic capital but also a history of connection with the military. IMPSA has played an important role in the country's military industry, especially by producing the sophisticated TAM tank, and has also participated actively in the country's nuclear plan (*Convicción*, Buenos Aires, January 4, 1981). In a political conjuncture when "geopolitical and strategic questions" were explicitly influential within the state bureaucracy, decision makers surely considered that an industry with a high strategic value should be protected. Another comparative advantage of the Argentine metallurgical industry over the construction industry was that contrary to Impregilo, Allis-Chalmers did not dominate the local electromechanical market of large-scale projects. Furthermore, Allis-Chalmers faced economic difficulties during this period that certainly, in comparison with Impregilo's stability, debilitated its position.

The consideration of the differences between the biddings of the YC-1 and the YE-1 contracts is relevant because they show how different industrial branches—and the related segments of a national bourgeoisie—may have different power vis-à-vis the state and international capital. The YC-1 contract shows a segment of the Argentine industrial bourgeoisie more vulnerable to foreign capital, in a subordinated position, given its relatively smaller power of negotiation. Generalizing from this example would take us close to a dependency approach. Dependistas tend to emphasize the vulnerability of local bourgeoisies because they are deeply marked by ideologies and theories of economic development that, in the 1950s and 1960s, stressed the need to strengthen Latin American national industrial bourgeoisies. Celso Furtado (1985), an active author in the development of dependistas interpretations clearly shows the origins of the dependency approach in CEPAL, the United Nation's Comisión Económica para la América Latina (Economic Commission for Latin America), in the 1950s, a time when industralization via import-substitution was a current perspective among Latin American elites.

But the YE-1 case shows another segment of the Argentine bourgeoisie that can compete with international capital and get a larger share. This case would lead us to a discussion closer to the post-dependency debate (see Becker 1983, 1984; Chase-Dunn 1982; Evans 1985), a debate that, in one sense, reflects more recent changes occurring within the most industrialized Latin American countries, and, in another, the influences of a world-system approach inspired in Immanuel Wallerstein's work (1974). Authors working in this direction did studies on industries with high capital concentration. Their efforts tended to emphasize the creation and operation of a powerful triangle formed by national capital, international capital, and the state. In these interpretations, national bourgeoisies are also seen as powerful actors that may define a situation on their own behalf.

The simultaneous consideration of the YC-1 and YE-1 contracts, however, with their typical negotiations between national and foreign capital, suggests that one segment of the bourgeoisie may act in ways that approximate a dependista model, while another bourgeois segment may follow avenues more in line with post-dependency patterns. This difference is due to the relative development of these factions of the bourgeoisie that, in turn, forms the basis of their separate negotiating power as compared with state and transnational capital.

The possibility of constructing a general interpretation for anticipating the behavior of the different actors involved in all bidding processes is extremely limited knowing that these processes are immediately sensitive to changing conditions of the national and international political economy. There is a common element that appears with regularity, however: the presence of consortia in all associative levels. I am going to argue that the common feature of all biddings is a process I call *consortiation.*

## Consortiation: Articulating Different Political/Economic Groups

The central importance of consortia for the development of large-scale projects is evident in Yacyretá. Consortia proliferate within the project, articulating a large number of transnational and nationally based corporations. The winner of the YC-1 contract is a consortium of thirty-two contractors from Italy, France, Germany, Argentina, Paraguay, and Uruguay. The winner of the YE-1 (turbines) contract is another consortium of German, Canadian, Argentine, and Paraguayan heavy industry corporations. Generators were awarded to a consortium led by Japanese corporations. The consultant's consortium is formed by American, German, Paraguayan, and Argentine firms. The infrastructure of the project on the work site, as well as the resettlement housing scheme was built by Argentine and Paraguayan consortia. Briefly, any relevant contract is submitted to a bidding process in which the participation of consortia predominates.

Indeed, a large-scale project such as Yacyretá is an arrangement of multiple segments of a centrally planned production process. Given the gigantism and internal differentiation of such projects, there is not a single corporation that can control all production processes involved in a project's completion. The project is thus divided into numerous segments that are offered in the market in the form of contracts to be awarded to several capitalist firms, the winners of different competitive bidding processes. At the same time, each separate contract, taken by itself, commonly represents a complex arrangement requiring and resulting in the combination of several firms. Therefore, a large-scale project is also a set of legal contracts that define different responsibilities and rewards for the participants. Association is a guiding principle that trickles down from the main contracts joining the largest international and national corporations to smaller ones where firms operating at local or regional markets become articulated with national corporations. I call this process through which a large-scale project promotes the articulation of different capitals *consortiation.*

Looking at Yacyretá as a whole, as a project where different capitalist firms became associated with one another to participate in the process, there is a line that clearly separates biddings where international and national capital form new consortia from those where only national participants are present. This differentiation is due not only to the technical complexities of the scale of the work (which may have a relatively less important weight), but also reflects exigencies and limitations introduced either by the international financing agencies (multilateral or export-financing banks) acting as brokers of transnational corporations or by the national state acting as a broker of national industry. I will come back to this point below.

In Yacyretá's largest bidding processes, such as those for the main civil works, turbines, and consultancy contracts, international capital participated in a leading position. The Argentine and Paraguayan corporations are the junior partners of these consortia. The part of the project that was left exclusively to national capital of both countries was the construction of the infrastructure works (housing and transportation system) and of the new housing related to the resettlement of the 40,000 people affected by the reservoir. Here Argentina and Paraguay clearly count on companies that are prepared for the development of the tasks as a whole. The argument that scale or technological complexity make obligatory the participation of international corporations cannot be applied to this situation. The different infrastructure works were thus carried out by consortia of leading national corporations.

The contracts related to the construction of new housing and urban equipment for the resettled population in Posadas (capital of the Argentine province of Misiones) are especially interesting in terms of illustrating the articulations of capitalist firms in consortia within Argentina. The scale of these jobs has been, for a period, an impediment for local-level (i.e., Posadas-based) construction companies, since they did not count on financial, managerial, and technological qualifications to win the contracts. The determining factor for the exclusion of local firms was the great number of houses to be constructed. In this context, the subordination of national capital to international capital within the main contracts is reproduced internally to Argentina. This time the terms of the contradiction were defined by the larger concentration of capital existing in the Great Buenos Aires area compared to the rest of Argentina. In consequence, powerful Buenos Aires–based construction companies dominated the contracts for the construction of the urban equipment of the resettlement segment of the project to the detriment of local-level firms.

This typically occurred during the military dictatorship (1976–83) when the prevailing economic policy was clearly biased toward the concentration of investments and procurements to the corporations operating at the level of the national market. After the new constitutional government's inauguration, the interaction of power groups was no longer exclusively limited to the rules dictated by monopolist capital.

One of the most frequent ways of legitimating a large-scale project is to praise its supposed positive effects on national as well as regional development. The clearest evidence of the democratic government's sensitivity to the claims of regional participation was its attempt to regionalize EBY's power structure (see chapter 2). Local- and regional-level firms could lobby the political administrative structures of their provinces. Regional participation, decentralization, became an issue. One solution was to offer the new housing contracts for the dislocated people in smaller lots that could allow the effective participation of the small, local, Posadas-based construction companies. But, at this level, consortiation also remained important. A leading Posadas firm formed a consortium with a Buenos Aires–based company, thus becoming the strongest participant in this segment of the larger investment that represents the Yacyretá project.

Consortiation is a chainlike movement that—through the organization of new task-oriented economic and administrative entities—actually links, within a project, international, national, and regional capitals. It is a way to reinforce capitalist relationships in a pyramidal fashion where upper levels hegemonize lower levels. The political-economic process of consortiation in large-scale projects directly affects the potential of such undertakings for socioeconomic development. Consortiation implies that such projects reinforce competition and the concentration of capital among capitalist firms; it facilitates the process of capital concentration by eliminating weaker competitors and co-opting a few selected ones.

If consortiation is a chainlike process that may reach the local level, it can be considered as involving a two-way process. On one hand, it allows selected smaller companies to participate as junior partners in tasks larger than what their financial, technological, and managerial capacities would allow. On the other hand, it is a way of facilitating the access of larger corporations to new and most often protected and highly disputed markets.

Through different discourses on a project's potential for regional and national development, the weakest partners in the associative chain legitimate their claims for larger participation. Regional development is thus a common argument of companies that operate at the local or regional level in their struggle against nationally based corporations. By the same token, national development is the argument national corporations use to defend their interests over international capital. Given the two-way characteristic of consortiation, the discourses on regional and national development may be an argument that the strongest partners, that is, those representing larger capital concentration, use to legitimate the need for the project. The eloquence of the developmental argument is evident when the co-optation of smaller unities down the scale is needed.

The vital importance of consortia for "macro-project development" has been pointed out before (Murphy 1983, 86). For Kathleen Murphy, a joint venture is a matter of a managerial rationale aimed at the sharing of risks and the increasing of the competitiveness of corporations. These features are presented as a result of a reading of market forces, where political power, or rather, power networking and negotiations do not seem to play any role. Nevertheless, the descriptions of Yacyretá's YC-1 and YE-1 cases make clear the importance of lobbying, power group pressures, and the incidence of political factors in the bidding processes as well as in the definition of the responsibilities and rewards of the consortia's members. Moreover, they indicate that the common presence of consortia in large-scale projects is a result of regulations both of the global market of large-scale projects by multilateral agencies and of nation-states to protect or stimulate different factions of national bourgeoisies. Consortia are a means that corporations have to optimize the use of different networks that must be activated for reaching different economic and political goals. For instance, a consortium operating at the conjunction of the international and national systems, and formed by national and transnational capital, may lobby both national and international-multilateral institutions.

Since there is not a transnational state, transnational capital influences world markets through multilateral agencies or creditors' cartels such as the Paris Club. The scale of the works and, more importantly, the rules of international financing give transnational corporations the lion's share of the total investments of a large-scale project. National corporations are given the possibility to participate in a greater or smaller degree within the ad hoc consortia according to their specific power connections and to the particularities of concrete political conjunctures informing the development policy of a nation-state.

Large-scale projects are unique opportunities to promote the articulation of international and national capital in a regulated environment under the supervision of different national states and supranational organizations. The consortium is the concrete social, economic, and political entity that operates this articulation. Forming a consortium always implies a negotiation that is a process based not only on economic or market criteria. The intervention of powerful actors—the owners or controllers of state, national, and transnational capital—generates a field of power negotiations that is eminently politically structured. Choosing national partners, for instance, is a strategic decision that takes into account that stronger political support within the national state may be more valued than other types of support. In fact, the definition of each company's share in a contract is due at least as much to political articulations, networkings, and lobbying as to the technical assessment of a company's technical, production, and financial capacity.

Consortia allow and legitimate the entrance of transnational capital in a national large-scale projects market. At the same time, they are part of the scenario (bidding conditions) where national corporations pressure the state to guarantee its share or a larger participation of a project's mass of investments. Finally, being the field where these interests are crossed, the state regulates and legitimates the final proportions of national capital participation, and the project as a whole, in the name of a given national development policy. The formation of consortia—marked by the strategic objective of winning a contract—thus promotes the articulation of transnational and national capitalist interests with those of managerial and political elites within the state. In this context, the limits to effective individual capitalist participation in the process of consortiation are defined by a complex combination of (a) access to technology, capital, and complex managerial processes, (b) the lobbying efficacy of a corporation's political networks, and (c) the kind of development policy stimulated by the state and by multilateral agencies.

# 4 The Moon Land:
## Yacyretá's Territorial Segmentation

Large-scale projects are world-system happenings that articulate *international* and *national* levels of integration but occur in *local* settings that are part of *regional* systems. Consequently, the characteristics of the participating population strongly reflect various levels of integration. Indeed, these projects create large labor forces that participate differently in labor markets formed by the junction of several class segments with different ethnic, migratory, ideological, and cultural backgrounds. A result of large-scale projects is to rearrange the previously existing local-space organization by creating settlement patterns for production needs. The internal differentiations of large-scale projects are translated into the concrete features of the settlement pattern of project territories. These features have important social determinants behind them and, at the same time, create new social constraints. I will describe the structure of social life in the area of the Yacyretá Project in order to elucidate the setting where actions unfold and the setting's importance for the perceptions that social actors have of each other's positions and privileges within Yacyretá's labor market (see figs. 2 and 4).

### The Moon Land: The Creation of Space for a Large-Scale Project

The Project's Immediate Area of Influence and Territory

The impact of large-scale projects in regional systems has been a major concern for Argentine social scientists and urban and regional planners. To determine the extent of the influence of Yacyretá, however, is not my goal here. Rather, I am concerned with the reality that the project creates and imposes on the territory. For analytical purposes, I will make an initial distinction between (a) the project's immediate area of influence, which includes the surrounding areas of the civil work's physical location that are not directly subordinated to Yacyretá and the future reservoir area with the population to be resettled, and (b) the project's territory, which includes the areas that are immediately geared to the construction activities or are directly influenced by the daily needs of the project's production process and social life.

Yacyretá's immediate area of influence covers a large surface of Paraguay and Argentina. In Paraguay, it includes part of the department of Itapúa, where most of the population to be resettled lives (especially in the city of Encarnación, Itapúa's capital), as well as part of the department of Misiones where construction site offices and the project's residential areas are located near the pre-existing town of Ayolas. On the Argentine shore, Yacyretá's direct area of influence also includes parts of two provinces, the politico-administrative units equivalent to Paraguayan departments. One is the province of Misiones. Its capital, Posadas, is inhabited by most of the Argentine population to be resettled. The other is the province of Corrientes where work site offices and Argentine residential areas are located near the pre-existing town of Ituzaingó.

A typical social impact analysis would focus on Yacyretá's immediate area of influence. Given my interest in understanding the project's internal characteristics, my main concern is on the project's territory. It is a set of areas either directly regulated by the needs of the project and its internal institutional power structure—the main contractor's permanent camps and the construction site, for example—or, as in the case of the two pre-existing towns, areas radically dependent on or subordinate to the project's political and economic power on a daily basis. I will consider Yacyretá's territory as the area that includes the construction site, the residential and service sectors directly linked to the project—that is, the two Villa Permanente and two 1,000 Viviendas camps on both shores of the river—as well as the towns of Ayolas (Paraguay) and Ituzaingó (Argentina).

The construction site, that is, the set of places where works such as the navigation locks, the powerhouse, and the spillways and dikes are constructed, comprises a distinct area within the project's territory. Besides the actual construction sites, some of the most important units related to the production process are located in this area: the main contractor's site office, the project's harbor, the cement and concrete plants, conveyor belts, workshops, garages, and so forth. A labor camp for Paraguayan unskilled workers is found on the island of Yacyretá. In Argentina a similar camp, the El Pinar camp, is located outside the work site area, five kilometers from its entrance.

Yacyretá, like many other geographic features in the region, is a guaraní name given by the pre-Columbian native population to the 450-square-kilometer island where the main facilities such as the project's powerhouse, are under construction. Yacyretá means "the moon land." The island is Paraguayan territory and divides the Paraná River into the Añá-Cuá and Principal branches. A service bridge constructed over the Principal branch links Argentine territory with the Paraguayan island of Yacyretá. Another bridge links the island to Paraguay's mainland.

These bridges create a physical connection between the two countries in that region. The construction site is not open to public access. Nonetheless, Argentine authorities have constantly reported the smuggling of commodities through the construction site. Indeed, contraband is a major political and economic force in Paraguay, a country known in the region for its smuggling of cigarettes, liquor, perfume, electric appliances, and Brazilian stolen cars. Reports of smuggling between the Paraguayan town of Ayolas and Argentine Ituzaingó were frequent (see, for instance, the article "Smuggling in Ituzaingó: The Investigation Goes On," in *El Litoral,* Corrientes, October 29, 1985; also *El Informador Público,* Buenos Aires, January 16, 1987).

The distinction between the construction site and the countryside is marked by the fence that surrounds it. There are only two road entrances to the project: one in Argentina, the other in Paraguay. Both of them are controlled either by Yacyretá's own security forces, by customs officers, or by the Army in Paraguay. The presence of Paraguayan soldiers carrying automatic weapons is visible at the Paraguayan entrance of the construction site as well as at various check points. Since the work site is a restricted area, access is permitted only to authorized vehicles belonging to the different corporations involved in the project.

The Yacyretá work site is a binational territory of 1,200 hectares where a set of protocols have been agreed upon between Paraguay and Argentina on matters such as the traffic of vehicles, customs, labor relations, and security and taxation. The protocols regulate the relationships between individuals, private firms, and the government agencies of both countries involved in the project (EBY 1986, 189–237). The main reason for these agreements was that the project is a unit, a special one from the juridical viewpoint since it represents a binational entity that cannot be treated only from a Paraguayan or Argentine legislative perspective. There was thus a need for common, uniform ways of solving problems to avoid constantly dealing with the specific legislation of each country.

The Yacyretá project clearly illustrates what I defined as one general feature of large-scale projects, *juridical ambiguity* (Ribeiro 1987), that is the creation of a specially regulated territory where the power of the main institutions involved in the production process can be stronger than the power of national states in those areas. Entidad Binacional Yacyretá, (EBY) for instance, has claimed its special juridical status to hinder the investigations of the Argentine attorney of National Administrative Investigations (Fiscalía Nacional de Investigaciones Administrativas) on mismanagement of public funds (*Revista Humor,* no. 157, 1985). In 1987, after threatening to confiscate the documents for which he was searching, the attorney was able to proceed with his investigations (*Revista Líder,* March 1987).

Given the binational character of Yacyretá, a residential or administrative infrastructure built on one side of the project had to be duplicated on the other side, in a mirrorlike structure. For example, one thousand houses were built to equip the main contractor's permanent camp on the Argentine side of the project. The same was done in Paraguay. The architecture of the residential and administrative buildings, however, differs on each side according to each country's architectural traditions.

Planners took advantage of the existence of two nineteenth-century towns in both countries, Ayolas and Ituzaingó, which were the bases for the construction period of the residential and transportation infrastructure of the project (see fig. 2). The history of Ayolas and Ituzaingó is intimately related to the Paraná River because for several decades they were the harbors that connected those then-remote Paraguayan and Argentine regions with markets as far as Buenos Aires and Asunción. These towns remain the only urban areas where a non-project-designed environment is available.

The following considerations are based on research conducted on the Argentine side of the project, where the largest concentration of project-engaged population is located. Research carried out on the Paraguayan side of the project, however, would reveal substantial descriptive and analytical differences due to Paraguay's position as a junior partner within the Yacyretá project as well as that country's different socioeconomic, political, and cultural reality. The expression "project's territory," when found in the text from this point on, will not include Yacyretá's residential areas in Paraguay or the nearby town of Ayolas. It will refer to the Argentine side of the project and the work sites.

## The Structure of Reproduction of Social Life in the Project's Territory

There is a basic distinction that needs to be introduced concerning the settlement pattern of the project's territory that was destined to the social reproduction of the population directly or indirectly related to the production process. This distinction refers to whether the spatial organization of the residential areas and the transportation system were designed by the project according to its internal conceptions and necessities or whether they refer to pre-existing settlement patterns that were rearranged or became a part of the project. Evidently, this distinction can only be made in historical terms because once a project is installed in an area it intervenes massively in the local settlement pattern, reorienting the spatial, social, and cultural characteristics previously in existence. This does not mean that pre-existing settlements totally lose their characteristics and importance, but they do undergo intense change provoked and almost always controlled by the external force represented by a project. Elsa Laurelli (1987) provides an interesting discussion on how large-scale projects in general affect regional settlement patterns.

The first distinction is in terms of defining two qualitatively different areas. One is a nonplanned environment, the pre-existing Correntino town of Ituzaingó, a nonproject-controlled area. The other is the project's planned housing and infrastructure equipment. This area, designed and controlled by Yacyretá, is divided into three main sections. The internal

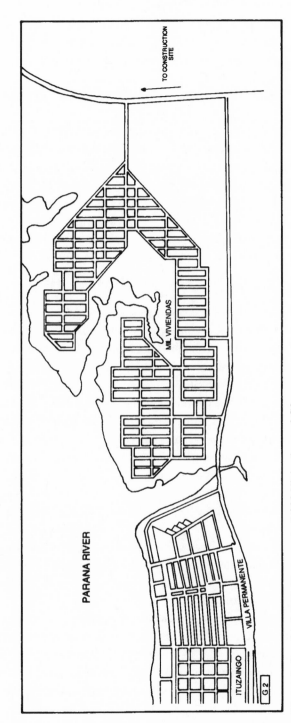

Figure 4. Ituzaingó, Villa Permanente, 1,000 Viviendas, and G2

characteristics of the Ituzaingó nonplanned area and the project's housing and infrastructure equipment are depicted next.

*The pueblo of Ituzaingó, province of Corrientes.* Ituzaingó is a small town, a pueblo, founded on the shore of the Paraná River in 1864 in the northeastern province of Corrientes. It is located at a distance of approximately 230 kilometers from the city of Corrientes, the province's capital, some 90 kilometers from Posadas, the capital of the neighboring province of Misiones, and almost 1,200 kilometers from the city of Buenos Aires, the federal capital.

Corrientes and Misiones, together with the provinces of Chaco and Formosa comprise the Argentine northeastern region. Since colonial times, Corrientes has been the most important province of the region. The power of Corrientes kept neighboring Misiones, for instance, under its political-administrative control until 1881 (Rofman 1983, 20). The founding of the city of Corrientes in 1588, at the junction of the Paraguay and Paraná rivers, was extremely important for the control and maintenance of these rivers' navigation routes (Romero 1986, 28).

Corrientes's unique political history as well as its distinct ethnic and cultural background clearly differentiates it from other members of the Argentine federation. The contradiction between *porteños* and correntinos is a historical issue that reflects the broad centralization of national political and economic power in the hands of Buenos Aires–based elites to the detriment of regional elites. The uneven exchange between Buenos Aires and Corrientes was aggravated during the military regime of 1976 to 1983 (Rofman et al. 1987).

Correntinos often refer to *centralismo porteño,* a major Argentine political issue, in terms of cultural incompatibilities. Indeed, in Corrientes bilingualism is common, since guaraní is widely spoken. Furthermore, for a long time the proximity to Paraguay, and especially to its capital, Asunción, once a most important colonial center, created strong ties between Correntinos and Paraguayans.

The economy of the province has been based historically on agricultural production and cattle ranching. Despite the importance of Corrientes' production of tobacco, rice, *yerba mate,* and cotton, its main individual source of wealth is cattle ranching. Data on Corrientes's gross product discriminated by sectors of economic activity and covering the 1970 to

1981 period, can be found in Rofman et al. (1987, 73). Cattle ranching based on large land holdings, with its associated gaucho culture, characterizes an extensive area of Corrientes, including its department of Ituzaingó, in the province's northeast, on the border of Misiones.

Seventy-five percent of Ituzaingó's area is dedicated to cattle ranching. The concentration of large landholdings in the hands of few characterizes the land tenure of the department (Provincia de Corrientes 1986, 25). The town of Ituzaingó has been the residence of the department's estancieros (cattle ranchers) and tradesmen, given its privileged location for the flow of commodities in the region.

Ituzaingó's history is intimately associated with the Paraná River, first, as an important regional harbor, and later, as the Argentine seat of the works of the Yacyretá project. The Apipé Rapids, located a few kilometers upstream from Ituzaingó, are the immediate reason for this town's existence and present importance. It was because of the Apipé Rapids that Ituzaingó became a harbor; it was necessary to channel the production of Misiones to the Buenos Aires and Asunción markets. It is also because of the Apipé Rapids that the Yacyretá Hydroelectric High Dam is being constructed, which is leading the pueblo of Ituzaingó to call itself the capital of energy.

The town was a harbor in the nineteenth century even before it was formally founded in 1864. In Corrientes the harbor of Ituzaingó is second only to the harbor of the province's capital. Almost 160,000 tons, mostly of construction materials, passed through it in the year of 1978. The town of Corrientes's harbor movement was of 177,542 tons in the same year (Provincia de Corrientes 1981, 173). The movement of passengers was also significant. Larger boats could not go farther than Ituzaingó where loads were transferred to smaller boats and taken to Posadas until the mid-1940s when the construction of a road, *Ruta Nacional* no. 12, between Corrientes and Posadas meant a strong competition for Ituzaingó's harbor. According to a local historian, Miguel Lopez Breard, during its busiest moments the harbor of Ituzaingó had thirty to forty boats at a time being loaded and unloaded. These tasks involved a considerable labor force. The importance of this transshipment harbor declined radically when *Ruta Nacional* no. 12 was paved in the 1960s.

Following the general trend of the province of Corrientes, Ituzaingó had high ratios of emigration until the 1970s. The evolution of Ituzaingó's ratios of emigration is the following (Meichtry 1978, 93):

| Years | Ratios (%) |
|-------|------------|
| 1946  | 10.1 |
| 1950  | 36.3 |
| 1955  | 35.9 |
| 1960  | 33.4 |
| 1965  | 29.6 |
| 1970  | 25.0 |

Migrants would most often go either to the province's capital or, following a general national trend, to the Greater Buenos Aires area.

During the 1970s, with the Yacyretá project, the pueblo underwent intense change in its demographic, social, and cultural composition. The population of the department of Ituzaingó that had been diminishing since the 1940s increased rapidly in the 1970s (Provincia de Corrientes 1981, 39): 1895, 3,292; 1914, 8,126; 1947, 14,278; 1960, 13,939; 1970, 13,502; 1980, 20,122.

Almost 60 percent of the department's population is urban. The town of Ituzaingó itself grew from 8,687 inhabitants in 1980 to 13,202 in 1984 (Provincia de Corrientes 1986, 7; 1984, 1).

Yacyretá's most intense impact on Ituzaingó must be understood in terms of two different periods: one related to the construction of the project's infrastructure (1978–83) and the period that began in early 1984, with the start of the main civil work and the arrival of the main contractor and its employees who occupied the housing infrastructure previously built. The relationship between the pueblo and project-generated social change varies according to each period.

Population growth was much stronger and more disorganized during the period of construction of the project's infrastructure (1978–83) and had heavier and more immediate social impact on the *Ituzaingueños* than after the beginning of the main civil works in 1984. One of the main reasons for this is because the initial stages of the project attracted a considerable amount of migrant labor that came to look for construction jobs or to participate in the economic boom that is supposed to accompany any large-scale project. Another reason is that the preliminary works of a project are destined to create the conditions to reproduce the large labor force that is to be engaged in the construction work. There was no pre-existing significant project housing infrastructure in Ituzaingó until

1981 when the Villa Permanente was opened. Before that, the project's employees—from the EBY and from the consultant firm (CIDY)—lived either in the town iself or in a small set of barracks, the Villa Transitoria, in the area that would later become the Villa Permanente. According to my informants, this Villa Transitoria was constructed in 1974.

The main residential infrastructure to be constructed was the 300 houses of EBY's Villa Permanente, and the 1,000 Viviendas permanent camp, 1,000 houses for the main contractor's labor force. In this period, workers were living in precarious temporary camps mostly located within Ituzaingó's limits or within walking distance. The constant and numerous presence of outsiders in the pueblo was thus much more intrusive than after the project's housing scheme was prepared. Permanent and temporary camps were built with many hundreds of houses, community centers, canteens, and educational, recreational, security, and health facilities. When the population to be engaged in the main civil work arrived, this infrastructure was ready. It must be noted that this migratory population is different from the one that participates at the construction of the project's infrastructure.

Although I was unable to find precise records on the total number of workers who participated in the construction of the infrastructure, I tend to agree with the most frequent evaluations that mention a maximum of 3,000 men. A study conducted in 1980 by the Buenos Aires office of the International Organization of Labor found the number of men working at the construction of the Villa Permanente to be 1,500 (Gaggiano 1980, 16). One of the first leaders of the local union of construction workers estimated that during the infrastructure construction the union had between 3,000 and 3,500 members. This seems to be a reasonable approximation for the number of men working during the peak moment of the preliminary works (1980–81) when the construction of the Villa Permanente (1978–81) overlapped with that of the 1,000 Viviendas (1980–82).

During the building of the infrastructure, there was a developmentalist boom in the town; small entrepreneurs made investments in the service sector, rents sky-rocketed, and a minilocalized inflation arose. The boom brought with it an excess male population who could not find either a job or a place to live. They had to either pay the extremely high rents that were being charged for beds in family houses, or join the growing number of homeless people sleeping on the town's plaza or streets. Squatting and prostitution became visible social issues, and so did public security.

The local representatives of the EBY and the several Argentine contractors, both with respective bodies of migrant labor they attracted for the construction of the infrastructure, were the main social actors involved in the conflicts and interactions that occurred between the Ituzaingueño population and project-related population. From the beginning, there developed a tension between task- and profit-oriented outsiders, who viewed the project as a moment in their search for upward social mobility, and local people. The local people also viewed the project as an economic opportunity for social mobility but at the same time, kept a sense of community, of belonging to a common local history and culture.

Conflict of interests generated by the project and its representatives was and still is often perceived as a confrontation between outsiders and local people. Furthermore, this confrontation develops within the larger context of the contradiction between national government and local people. In Argentina, federal power means Buenos Aires's political and economic power. The outsiders versus local people issue, created by the Yacyretá project, soon came to be represented in terms of porteños versus correntinos. Prejudice and discrimination against people from provinces such as Corrientes is part of the ideology of some sectors of the Buenos Aires population. *Cabecita negra,* "black little head," is the label the chiefly European descended porteños coined to classify migrants coming from different regions of the country (Ratier 1971). The Argentine national headquarters of EBY is in Buenos Aires, permanently imparting to the EBY an undisputed porteño flavor.

The local population predating the project may be placed in a subordinated position, but it is not totally devoid of power. Actually, this depends strongly on the kinds of interactions that different segments of the pueblo, especially the local elite, develop with the project structure. Yacyretá is the strongest source of social power in the area. Members of the local elite, politicians and merchants, for instance, have also been co-opted by Yacyretá either by becoming participants of the project's local bureaucracy or by selling it services.

The integration of Ituzaingueños with project-related people has been until the present an important issue in the area. Since the construction of the project's infrastructure, local people started to protest against what was seen as the creation of two Ituzaingós: one, the historic, poor Ituzaingó, represented by Correntinos that were mostly hired as unskilled laborers by the Yacyretá project; the other, the new, powerful, national, and international Ituzaingó, geared to the binational hydroelectric dam, the project that soon became the most important economic and political force in the region.

The decision on the location of Yacyretá's housing infrastructure was perhaps one of the most important ones in which the province of Corrientes could take an active part. During the Peronist government of 1973–76, a mixed EBY/Provincia de Corrientes committee was established to make decisions on this subject. According to an Ituzaingueño politician, a former member of this committee, the EBY tended to foster the construction of camps at a distance of more than ten kilometers from the town of Ituzaingó. Through the initiative of the Correntino politicians, this idea was abandoned in favor of the urbanistic integration of the historic settlement with the new ones to be constructed.

In fact, the Villa Permanente, a housing area for EBY's personnel, began to be constructed in a peripheral area contiguous to Ituzaingó in 1978. For its construction, 270 Ituzaingueño families had to be resettled: 68 percent of them were squatters living in ranchos, precarious dwellings where they could have small animals and could plant some important staples, such as manioc, corn, and several fruits in the backyard (Provincia de Corrientes 1980a). They were characterized as a semirural population who did odd jobs for either the cattle ranchers or the town's dwellers. After the resettlement, they were increasingly recruited to work at the construction of the project's infrastructure (Provincia de Corrientes 1978, 1980b).

They were resettled in another area of the town where the poorly built 180 Viviendas housing project was erected by the government of the province of Corrientes. Residents of the 180 Viviendas frequently complained of the bad quality of the houses and of the small size of the lots where they could not plant vegetables or keep as many animals as before (*El Litoral,* Corrientes, August 28, 1980). Indeed, the loss of part of the peasants' fund of subsistence represented by domestic animals and small gardens, is known to be one of the negative impacts on populations undergoing processes of proletarianization caused by forced resettlement (Sigaud 1986).

An issue that clearly illustrated the tension between local people and outsiders arose in early 1981 when the Villa Permanente began to be inhabited. In this area, approximately 300 houses for urban professionals were erected. After the construction period, the fence that was built to cordon the construction site was not demolished. This new housing area became in practice a semiprivate tract of land owned by the Argentine federal government. The Villa Permanente had only two entrances where Ituzaingueños had to identify themselves and tell where they were going before being allowed to get in the area. This created intense resentment because the Ituzaingueños considered the villa as part of their town and they felt humiliated by the fence. Some of them called it the Berlin Wall, a symbol of porteño arrogance and disdain; others regarded it as an index of the degree of militarization that Argentine society was undergoing during the dictatorship of 1976–83.

Both judgments were partially right. The security of the project's residential area is, in last instance, the responsibility of the federal government. Nevertheless, the Villa Permanente, with its brand-new comfortable modern houses, was being occupied by professionals, managers, and highly trained technicians transferred from the Buenos Aires headquarters of the EBY to the work site. Most of these were receiving wages and enjoying a style of consumption that they would not have in metropolitan Buenos Aires. Many of these professionals held pejorative views of Correntinos as "feudal" and backward when compared to the modern, European-like Buenos Aires life. Briefly, the Villa Permanente represented a sparkling architectural, class, and cultural contrast beside the old, historic, Correntino Ituzaingó.

In September 1981, following the increasing protests of local leaders, the "Berlin Wall" was finally torn down. *El Litoral,* a newspaper based in the city of Corrientes, the province's capital, wrote that this was the end of "the two Ituzaingós, in which the native inhabitants living in the old town seemed to be relegated to a condition of second-class citizens, characterizing a sort of unusual discrimination" (*El Litoral,* Corrientes, September 15, 1981). The fence, however, symbolized an objective distinction. Historic Ituzaingó is a heterogenous urban space that kept its overall pueblo appearance with its local architecture and unpaved streets. The pueblo's urban services, such as sewage, public lighting, and telephone, although highly improved—and sometimes installed with the arrival of the project—cannot be compared to those at Villa Permanente. The latter is a homogeneous urban professional housing area, presently separated from the rest of the town by a paved street, a line that represents, to use a local

expression, a mental wall. The interaction between outsiders and Ituzaingueños remains problematic and subject to the mutually biased perception
of porteño and correntino identities, as well as to differences in the access
to the main power structure operating in the area: the Yacyretá project.

This framework is partially valid in helping to understand the relationships between local people and an important institution that established
itself within the area of historic Ituzaingó: the union of construction
workers. Ituzaingueños view the union as an institution linked mostly to
the national power sphere. Union leaders view Ituzaingó as an old Correntino cattle-ranching pueblo that has not yet left its traditional past
behind and has never understood what the presence of the Yacyretá project
implied. The UOCRA, *Unión de los Obreros de la Construcción de la
República Argentina* (Union of the Construction Workers of the Argentine
Republic), opened its local in Ituzaingó in 1977 in response to the growing
number of workers arriving for the preparation of the infrastructure construction. One of its first leaders described several wildcat strikes during
this construction. These confrontations were mostly due to delays in
workers' payments and they happened during the military dictatorship of
1976–83, a particularly difficult time for the Argentine labor movement.

The increase of such a large number of men to Ituzaingó's population
brought other changes besides the UOCRA's presence. Many of the
newcomers were part of a migratory labor system (Burawoy 1976), a
typical situation for the unskilled segment of large-scale project labor
markets that is basically composed of men not accompanied by their
families (Ribeiro 1987). Not all of these men were living in contractors'
temporary camps. Those who could not afford the extremely high rents
lived either on the streets of Ituzaingó or squatted in the periphery of the
town. The great number of men constituted an unusual demographic
pressure on the town. Prostitution flourished. But new families were
created. The demographic dynamics of the town were already intimately
related to the quality, rhythm, and intensity of investments made by the
Yacyretá project in the area.

After the peak period of construction of the Villa Permanente (1978–81)
and of the 1,000 Viviendas (September 1980–December 1982), there was
a lessening of activities that lasted until the mobilization of the main
contractor's labor force in early 1984. This critical period began to unfold
with the political changes in Argentina's national government represented

by the advent to power of General Galtieri (December 1981) and the budget restrictions his government imposed. The federal government was not sensitive to the mobilization of the local and regional population for the continued support of the rhythms of investment in the area. The situation strongly deteriorated during the Malvinas War period (April 1982–June 1982). With the sharp decline of the construction activity, the end of the building of the 1,000 Viviendas (December 1982), and the uncertainty of the project's future, contractors, and the jobs they represented, left the area.

Consequently, many men abandoned the families they had recently formed. According to the Ituzaingueños, this situation created a significant number of matrifocal families, especially on the periphery of historic Ituzaingó. Indeed, out of 2,405 Ituzaingueño families, 321 were headed by women (Provincia de Corrientes 1984, 57). As part of a discussion both on the consequences of the period of construction of the infrastructure and the lack of adequate preparation of the local population for project-related social change, on December 4, 1984, *El Litoral,* the newspaper from the city of Corrientes, published the following considerations: "When there were almost 5,000 workers [in Ituzaingó], although there was a red-light district especially designed for this male population of outsiders, many men preferred the "stability" of other relationships, that, of course, would be temporary. They created real families that were soon to be abandoned to their own fate. There also were many births. Consequently, mothers and children were abandoned, generating, in many cases, true social dramas."

From 1982 to 1983, when the fate of the main civil works contract was uncertain, was a period of stagnation that represented the end of a developmental cycle created by the Yacyretá project. This period vividly demonstrated not only the subordination of the local population to the project's dynamics defined at the national level, but also the end of the expectations of steady progress created around Yacyretá by different national and regional agencies. In official assessments on the potential impact of the project, a need for new investments in services was identified. Ultimately, this represented one way through which expectations that could not be fulfilled were created (see, for instance, Provincia de Corrientes n.d.). These expectations had given rise to a flow of people into service businesses, a dream of success that did not materialize. According to a former president of Ituzaingó's Chamber of Commerce, many small entrepreneurs, who were attracted by the discourse on regional development, went into bankruptcy. These expectations were stimulated by the developmentalist/modernizing discourses commonly attached to large-scale projects.

On January 26, 1982, *El Litoral* published an article entitled "The Delays in EBY's Timetable Generates Problems." Its main comments were the following: "The complaints brought to this paper are endless. The state is reproached for having called up entrepreneurs, tradesmen and producers to invest to start the development of Ituzaingó following the undertaking, but now does not respond to the expectations that it has itself provoked . . . it seems that the government does not care about the risks that are being taken by many people who had believed in its announcements, in a work that should never be paralyzed like now, generating losses. This is the general opinion in Ituzaingó. The activity has decreased totally. There are stores that scarcely sell. Other stores, especially those owned by newcomers, had to close."

The relationship between Ituzaingó and the Yacyretá project changed substantially after the arrival of ERIDAY, the main contractor, in early 1984. The housing infrastructure was ready and the town's urban structure did not feel the intensity of demographic pressure as it previously had. A transportation system was established by ERIDAY. Buses began taking workers and administrative personnel from different residential areas— including Ituzaingó and its periphery—to the work site, thus detouring the flow of pedestrians away from the pueblo.

The internal differentiation of ERIDAY's transportation system reflected the labor market's hierarchy. The company provided its managers, professionals, and technicians with pickups and cars that were also used for personal purposes. The quality of buses varied according to the riders' positions in the labor market. Administrative personnel used smaller and more comfortable buses than workers, for instance. The buses provided by ERIDAY were free and they connected all residential areas of the project including the pueblo of Ituzaingó. They were also used by the local population.

In this new situation, a most important factor was that the El Pinar camp, the residential area of the main contractor's unskilled labor force, that is, male workers unaccompanied by their families, was located ten kilometers away from Ituzaingó. Furthermore, one of the first works built by ERIDAY was a bridge, open to traffic in 1985, on the Paraná River's main branch between Argentine territory and Yacyretá Island, thus completing a crucial road connection between Argentina and the main work sites in Paraguayan territory. Argentine workers then had the opportunity to go across Ya-cyretá Island to Paraguay's mainland, since the bridge over the Añá-Cuá branch had been put in service in 1983.

This road connection is another factor that contributed to a substantial reduction of the pressures from the presence of the increased number of men in the population in Ituzaingó. Workers were now able to cross to Paraguay, where commodities and services were cheaper than in Argentina, and spend their money in Paraguayan bars and brothels. A night in the red-light district could cost almost four times less on the Paraguayan side than in Argentina. But Paraguayan prostitutes also could cross to Argentina on a regular basis.

The main contractor not only employed a large and growing labor force, but also managed—and manages—most of the resources directly involved in the construction project. After the arrival of ERIDAY, some of the most important issues affecting Ituzaingó—such as the conservation of its infrastructure, the integration of the different sectors now forming the town, and the adequate attention to education and health matters—became related to the increasing presence and power of ERIDAY in the area. For Ituzaingu.eños EBY was no longer the only interlocutor. The solution for Ituzaingó's problems now had to be sought primarily through tripartite negotiations involving the town's politicians, the EBY, and ERIDAY.

*Project housing and infrastructure equipment.* The construction of the infrastructure (1978–83) was used by Argentine authorities as a testimony that despite the prolonged uncertainty about the awarding of the main civil works contract, Yacyretá was slowly but concretely being carried out. The infrastructure work became a subject of controversy in Argentina due to the high costs of the housing projects and the luxurious quality of some of the units destined for the absentee directors of EBY. In Villa Permanente there is an area of twenty-eight houses, designed for Argentine EBY's managers, that were never occupied and remained empty at least until 1987. On the Paraguayan side of the project there is an exclusive villa, surrounded by gardens and a fence, where six luxurious houses remain at the disposal of directors, high-level officials, and VIP visitors.

The Argentine press frequently alluded to the price of "camp houses" that cost many times more than comfortable apartments in *Barrio Norte,* an elegant section of Buenos Aires. On August 14, 1981, *La Prensa* printed: "In Ituzaingó a village of 300 houses is about to be finished for the amount of U.S.$170–90 million. But the EBY's employees are not going to be the only people to have a house granted. For each director of that organism, for instance, the construction of a modest U.S.$500 thousand chalet is foreseen, a cost that does not include, for sure, the price of the infrastructure, or, perhaps, that of the sauna."

The main housing areas that were planned and constructed in the Argentine territory because of the project are the Villa Permanente, the 1,000 Viviendas, and the El Pinar camp. There is also a compound built only for the main contractor's unmarried administrative staff, called the G2 camp, located nearby Ituzaingó. Equivalent housing projects were constructed on the Paraguayan side of the project. The totality of the project's housing occupied by the main contractor and its subcontractors has been divided into eight groups classified as G1, G2, and so forth until G8. But, I will not describe the G2 camp or the infrastructure located within the construction site such as the project's harbor and administrative quarters, canteens, workshops, and cement and concrete plants.

In Ituzaingó's area, Argentine contractors built the housing projects and the main urban infrastructure equipment—such as a water purification plant, a sewer treatment plant, and a thermoelectric power plant—with the capacity to attend the pueblo and the three project-constructed housing areas. In Ituzaingó's main plaza, a "cultural center" was built and the town's Catholic church was renovated by the project. Preliminary works also included the construction (1979–83) of a major bridge on the Añá-Cuá branch of the Paraná River, linking the Yacyretá Island to Paraguay's mainland.

A description of the Villa Permanente, the Mil Viviendas, and the El Pinar encampment will outline the labor market segmentation and hierarchical organization of Yacyretá, issues that are going to be discussed in detail in the next chapter. A characterization of the planned settlement pattern will show clearly how the project's internal stratification is translated into spatial realities. In fact, these housing projects are sui generis residential areas prepared for Yacyretá's managerial elite (Villa Permanente), middle class and skilled workers (1,000 Viviendas), and unskilled workers (El Pinar camp). Their locations were defined within a field of tensions where the main poles of attraction were the pueblo of Ituzaingó and the hydroelectric dam construction site. These two places are fifteen kilometers apart. The following sections will make clear that the rationale governing the urban and architectural project is class-biased.

## The Villa Permanente

The Villa Permanente is a set of 300 houses constructed between 1978 and 1981 in an area contiguous to Ituzaingó for the elite of the Yacyretá project. Although Villa Permanente was completed in 1982 (Summa 1984), I am considering 1981 as the year it was completed because this was when the housing project began to be inhabited. Before its opening, a small number of EBY's employees lived first in the pueblo and later in the Villa Transitoria, a simpler and more camplike area that is currently part of the Villa Permanente and inhabited by the EBY's rank and file personnel.

Until 1984, with the arrival of the main contractor's labor force, the Villa Permanente was the main area inhabited by project-related personnel. It is located at a distance of some fifteen kilometers from the construction site. During the construction period it will house the personnel of EBY (the vast majority of its dwellers), of the consultant (CIDY), and the top managers of the main contractor (ERIDAY). Once the project is completed it will house the people responsible for the operation of the hydroelectric dam.

The area is administered by EBY. Its security is provided by the Argentine National Guard, which has a·guard post right at the beginning of the paved road that marks the separation between the Villa and the pueblo of Ituzaingó.

The main offices of EBY and CIDY in the project's area were located in the Villa Permanente until 1986/1987, when they were almost entirely transferred to the work site. The public relations office for EBY, the most important institutional interface with the general public (most often tourists and students attracted by the project) is also located in the Villa Permanente.

An elementary school that serves both the Villa and Ituzaingó was built on the banks of the Paraná. By the riverside, there is a large three-story building that at the same time is a lodging for EBY's single personnel (pabellón de solteros), a hotel for visitors, and a club with a restaurant and a bar where the project's elite meet. These facilities also include a swimming pool and basketball and volleyball quarters that are usually empty. Another building that was constructed to be a hotel, also by the river, has been finished for some years but remained closed at least until 1987. The appearance of emptiness is a quality shared by the whole area of the Villa Permanente which is invariably deserted. To analyze why the use of public space is so limited in this housing project I need to advance further in the description of its overall social composition.

Most of Villa Permanente's inhabitants are Argentine administrative personnel, technicians, and professionals transferred from Buenos Aires with their families. A segment of the Villa's population came from the city of Corrientes in the period the project was run by a Correntino executive director (December 1983–June 1985). Although under the new management there began a steady erosion of this group's political-administrative power, it remained an important identifiable network. A small number of foreigners, the top on-site managers of the consultant and of the main contractor, also live in Villa Permanente.

Despite the fact that the Villa's inhabitants are the project's elite, they share with other segments of Yacyretá's labor market a central characteristic of their social experience: they are migrant labor. But, being "uprooted," a label constantly used to classify this situation, is experienced differently according to one's occupational and migratory background. An engineer who has participated in several construction projects in different geographical contexts and who is used to suburban or small-village social experiences is less likely to suffer from the isolation and loss of his previous social networks than a lawyer transferred directly from metropolitan Buenos Aires. The complex issues involved in the relationships between migratory experience and labor market segmentation will be explored in chapter 5.

Social integration is an issue in this community of migrants. Indeed, despite organized efforts, for the Villa Permanente inhabitants, the household has become the focus of their daily lives. The sense of community-oriented life has deteriorated due to the overlapping of the residential space with the working space. Dwellers of the Villa, especially those working for EBY, that is, the majority, agree that living there means never leaving your work environment. In fact, most of the offices can be reached in a walk of five to ten minutes from any house in the Villa. More importantly, office hierarchy and daily workplace relationships mark the interactions between neighbors in the area. The general assessment is that labor-related conflicts ultimately invade the totality of social interactions, thus influencing the mutual perceptions of individuals.

In this connection, Villa Permanente's public space has been strongly conditioned by the logic of the production activity, not only because it was a space designed as part of a larger planned production scheme, but mainly because daily labor relationships have migrated from the workplace to the residential area. Activities conceived to develop a notion of *communitas,* such as sports tournaments, are, nonetheless, still informed by the same principle. The teams of a volleyball championship organized in 1986 mirrored the organization chart of EBY. On a given night, the Technical Department might play against Public Relations, or Security against Personnel.

In previous works (Ribeiro 1980, 1987), I suggested that social life in large-scale projects housing areas, especially in workers' camps, might well fit the notion of a total institution (Goffman 1962) where the power of a central administration regulated individuals' daily activities. In Yacyretá, as in other large-scale projects, housing is also a fringe benefit, a compensation for environmental and social hardships. In fact, the project grants not only rent-free housing but also standardized furniture. This ultimately restrains the possibility of individualization, creating a uniform appearance of private spaces, reinforced by the homogeneous architecture of the housing project. This creates the perception of living in a monotonous, steady world where one never leaves work.

The appearance of emptiness of the public space, epitomized by a clean and attractive but nonetheless unattended leisure area, is, in last instance, a consequence of the organization of production that ultimately subordinates other spheres of social life to its own logic, inhibitting the development of project-free social interactions. Villa Permanente is experienced as a community closed in on itself where the reproduction of social daily life—with its basic implications for the predictability, monitoring, and attribution of individuals' positions—is directly referred to the bureaucratic power structure of the Yacyretá project. For the small population of Villa Permanente, social control is potentially, and sometimes virtually, intertwined with labor control. As one employee of EBY said, ''You don't go to the club's swimming pool because you do not want to see the same office faces, or, what is worse, a hierarchical superior with whom you have been developing disagreements.''

"Golden Cage": this is how a high-level official characterized the Villa Permanente in a shrewd assessment of the ambiguous situation of being in a privileged position within Yacyretá's hierarchical structure and, at the same time, leading a limited daily social life.

### The 1,000 Viviendas

The 1,000 Viviendas constitutes a whole compound in itself, independent of other residential areas in the Yacyretá project area. As its name indicates this is a housing project of one thousand houses. Las mil (the one thousand), as it is informally called, was constructed between September 1980 and December 1982 to lodge the main contractor's skilled labor force during the construction of the main civil works. Designed to last fifty years, its destiny after the project's completion is uncertain and represents a major concern for local politicians. It is separated from Villa Permanente by a ditch and is approximately fourteen kilometers away from the work site. Las mil is where most of the Argentine population of the Yacyretá project lives. In June 1986, 905 of its houses were occupied, 90 percent (816) by ERIDAY's employees.

There are two main types of residence in the 1,000 Viviendas. The number of bedrooms may vary internally within each type, but the immediate distinction between them is roof color. This difference operates as an index of ERIDAY's internal stratification. Red-roofed houses are larger and are occupied by persons in higher positions within ERIDAY's hierarchical structure. These houses are not grouped in any special section of the 1,000 Viviendas. Their tenants are professionals, highly skilled technicians, and managers. Grey-roofed houses, the majority, are smaller and in general are inhabited by skilled workers and service and administrative personnel.

The 1,000 Viviendas has a service center where there is a branch of the Banco de la Provincia de Corrientes, a post-office, newsstands, stores, and a complete supermarket run by ERIDAY, which is open to the general public. This supermarket has been a focus of contentions; it is one facet of what may be called the "developmental contradictions" of the Yacyretá project. The supermarket benefits from the exemption of federal taxes that covers all transactions involved with the project. The prices of the products it sells, however, do not reflect this tax exemption. On one hand, the supermarket has released workers and the Ituzaingueño population from the weight of local commercial speculation and overpricing caused by the presence of the project. But the fact that the supermarket's prices are not discount values still means for most of the project-related population that the main contractor is making profits by selling goods subsidized by the federal government. On the other hand, local retailers and entrepreneurs, one of the local groups supposed to benefit from project's presence, claim that they cannot compete with a powerful seller that buys in large quantities in Buenos Aires markets.

Other major structures of the 1,000 Viviendas consist of a church near the service center, a club with facilities that include a large swimming pool, and the barracks of the Argentine National Guard, the federal force responsible for the project's security. One of the houses of this residential area is the local seat of UDEGOC, Unión de los Empleados en Grandes Obras y Conexas (Union of the Employees in Great Works and Connected). In contrast to the UOCRA-Ituzaingó (the union of construction workers that are paid on an hourly basis), UDEGOC represents the part of the main contractor's labor force that receives monthly wages. The segments of the labor market covered by UDEGOC range from skilled workers to foremen and engineers.

In comparison to the Villa Permanente, the 1,000 Viviendas housing project is neither marked by the constant presence and power of the EBY nor by a conflictive history with the pueblo of Ituzaingó. At the same time, both its greater size and its more heterogeneous social composition seem to have significantly reduced the totalizing connotations of the "Golden Cage." Public space is not as deserted as in the Villa Permanente giving to the One Thousand an appearance of greater sociability.

There are two basic cleavages within the social composition of the 1,000 Viviendas population, both related to structural characteristics of the labor market. The first division distinguishes production controllers from workers. Professionals, managers, highly specialized technicians, and foremen live in the same area with skilled workers, but, as described before, in different types of houses. A second division distinguishes the national Argentine population from the European. The Argentine population, the vast majority in the area, is segmented by provincial origin. The composition of the European population parallels the internal contractual divisions of the ERIDAY consortium. The European personnel of the main contractor is basically divided into Italians and French who, in February 1986, represented 59.3 percent and 32.1 percent, respectively; that is, 91.4 percent of a total of 140 Europeans in the area of the work site.

In Yacyretá, the European population is mixed with the local national population. European quarters are a common part of large-scale projects worldwide. The absence of an exclusive European compound is a cause of resentment for many Europeans who were used to previous experiences where they had housing privileges based on racial and ethnic differences. According to an Italian manager, in comparison to other projects where he had previously lived, both in South America and in Africa, the 1,000 Viviendas settlement pattern is more classist than racist.

Although Yacyretá's settlement pattern does not reproduce the colonial foreigners/natives separation, in it there can be found a reminiscence of this "colonial bias" that has caused resentments, this time amongst the Argentine population. In an isolated area located some kilometers far from the 1,000 Viviendas, there is a Club Hípico (equestrian club) where the European population of the project, especially its most powerful members, keeps horses and gives parties. Although the entrance of Argentines is not forbidden, this club is in fact only open to Europeans. Several of the gatherings are ethnically informed celebrations, and some of the few Argentines who have been invited to the club felt discriminated against. Here the ethnic line clearly crosses with the internal power hierarchy of the project. In such an arena, Europeans may perform rituals to reinforce their ethnic identities free from exposures or perceptions that could lead to "misreadings" capable of calling into question their power positions within the project. Indeed, ethnicity is an issue in the 1,000 Viviendas and in the Yacyretá project as a whole, since for most of the pressing problems at work—labor relations, for instance—Europeans are decisive power holders. In this connection, class and labor conflicts tend to be perceived also in terms of ethnicity. Moreover, since Europeans are a closed power elite within the project, the club is also an arena where top managers may engage in joking relationships, in rituals that temporarily dissolve differences defined by the workplace, but that at the same time reinforce their unity as a power group vis-à-vis other power groups.

Another important marker of the presence of ethnicity as an issue in the 1,000 Viviendas refers to the educational structure of this housing project. The ethnic segmentation of the labor market is reflected directly in the educational system. Of great importance for the understanding of the 1,000 Vivienda's community are the three schools that serve its children. The largest of them is a public elementary school for the children of ERIDAY's Argentine employees. The two others are Italian and French schools for the children of ERIDAY's European employees. The institutional and pedagogic organization of these schools observes Argentine, Italian, and French standards of formal education, respectively. There was also a German "school," consisting of a classroom with five children in different grades, located within the Italian school building. The importance of schools for the maintenance of the main contractor's skilled labor force is considered in the next chapter.

Both EBY and ERIDAY are influential in the school system of the project as a whole. The school system of the Yacyretá territory in Argentina includes a project-built kindergarten and elementary school on the border of Ituzaingó and Villa Permanente. An older Ituzaingueño high school and a few other elementary schools receive some support from the EBY. The main contractor, ERIDAY, and EBY may provide either institutional support, acting as a liaison with, for instance, regional or national educational organisms, or material aid, such as grants, minor construction, and maintenance works in school facilities. At the work site EBY has a small staff, headed by a person with a B.A. in Education, that struggles with a chronic lack of funds to deal with the numerous, complicated educational problems of the local schools.

The Argentine school at the 1,000 Viviendas is managed by the province of Corrientes with additional economic and orientational assistance from EBY and eventually ERIDAY will supply material support. From early 1984, when it was opened to the children of ERIDAY's skilled labor force, until 1986, the number of its students tripled. In March 1986, at the beginning of the school year, 774 children were matriculated. As of September 1984, out of 557 students, the single largest group came from the province of Corrientes (26 percent), followed by children from Entre Ríos (16.7 percent) and Neuquén (12 percent). These data correspond to students' origins that do not necessarily coincide with their place of birth. Sixteen other Argentine provinces were represented in the students' population. There were also forty-one children from four South American countries: Paraguay, Uruguay, Venezuela, and Peru. Uruguayans made up 83 percent of the latter group.

The heterogeneity of the provincial and national origins of students as well as the unusual rate of weekly admissions are the most challenging difficulties faced by the Argentine school. The number of different curricular backgrounds of the children and a constantly growing number of students per classroom are problems that are reflections of the dynamics of Yacyretá's labor market formation. The growth of the main contractor's labor force is expectedly intense in the first years of a project's execution. Correntinos apart, the largest groups of children quoted above came with their families from Salto Grande and Alicurá, other hydroelectric dams erected by Impregilo, the lead firm of ERIDAY's consortium. Salto Grande is a binational project constructed on the border of the Argentine province of Entre Ríos and Uruguay, while Alicurá was constructed in the province of Neuquén.

The Scuola Italiana Cisalpina di Yacyretá is the largest of the European schools of 1,000 Viviendas. It is directly linked to the general services that Impregilo, the Italian contractor, provides for its personnel. Scuolas are common in the large-scale projects where Impregilo participates in different areas of the world; some are larger than the one at Yacyretá. These schools are part of the services that major international contractors need to offer if they want to maintain their skilled labor force on a world scale.

At scuolas, the school year follows the Italian calendar, starting when it is fall in Europe and spring in Argentina. Perhaps the most important reason for the observance of the Italian calendar is to prevent mistimed transferences of students to other Italian schools located either at home or at a different work site abroad. In September 1985, the beginning of the 1985–86 school year, the Scuola Italiana Cisalpina di Yacyretá had sixty-two students distributed in all different grade levels of the Italian pre-university educational system, ranging from kindergarten to *liceo*. The sixty-two students were distributed as follows: *asilo,* 12; *prescolare,* 7; *elementare,* 18; *media,* 14; and *liceo,* 11.

The fact that the school's activities are programmed according to the Italian school calendar creates a sort of anachronism, a temporal mismatch indicative of the cultural ambiguities experienced by teachers and students. The seasonal cycles of the Southern hemisphere are the opposite of those in the Northern hemisphere. When Argentine children are having summertime vacation, Yacyretá's Italian children are going to school as if they were in their home country. Accordingly, after a geography class on the characteristics of winter and mountain life in Italy, children go home in a hot, humid Southern hemisphere summer day in Corrientes's flatlands. Indeed, cultural ambivalence is a problem that teachers face in the school. Students are taught *as if* they were in Italy, but, commented a teacher, when they open the door of the school, they find themselves in a work site community in the northeast of Argentina on the border of Paraguay.

The scuola's children also experience a bilingual environment, primarily because Spanish is the predominant language used in the vast majority of public spaces. At the same time, their homes are usually attended by Spanish-speaking Argentine maids. Local television is also in Spanish. Furthermore, binational couples are common within the project's European population. I was not able to determine the number of Italian–Latin American couples, however. Nevertheless, children born in Spanish-speaking South American countries represented 36.5 percent of the total number of registered students for the 1986–87 school year. That does not mean, though, that all of them are children of Italian–Latin American couples. But, the mothers of some of these children are Spanish-speaking natives because several younger Italian technicians and professionals working for Impregilo have married Uruguayan women during the construction of the Salto Grande Argentine-Uruguayan dam. Spanish was thus the first language for a small but significant number of children, while Italian was learned at school as a second language.

Cultural ambiguity, that is, the simultaneous experiencing of different systems of signs and practices, ultimately has invaded not only the classes of geography, but also those of writing and reading. Indeed, being ''neither fish nor meat''—to use the Italian expression describing this situation—is a major characteristic of the social lives of the European population in Yacyretá.

### The El Pinar Camp

El Pinar is the name workers gave to the Rincón Santa María camp, or G3, because of a pine woodland that exists near the area. It is a compound of forty-two dormitories with a total of 2,688 places available for the unskilled labor force. In each two-story building there are sixteen bedrooms per floor and four bathrooms at the end of each floor. Stores, offices, a first-aid station, and a large mess hall with its own industrial kitchen are also part of this housing project.

Construction for this camp began in August 1984. Almost two years passed between the arrival of the main contractor at the construction site in early 1984 and the opening of the El Pinar camp in late 1985. There are indications that in this interval there was no appropriate housing for the unskilled segment of the labor force of the project as a whole. Indeed, an Asunción paper published news on Paraguayan workers protesting the housing conditions before the opening of project's labor camps (*Última Hora,* March 27, 1985).

By June 1986, there were 915 men living in El Pinar. In this same month there were 826 men living in the Isla Yacyretá labor camp on Paraguayan territory. The total population of workers living in Yacyretá project's labor camps was 1,741 men, that is, 51 percent of the total number of persons (3,354) living in the residential areas managed by the main contractor. In that same month there were 4,958 persons working for ERIDAY and its subcontractors.

El Pinar is classified as a residential area for single unskilled workers despite the fact that many of its inhabitants are married men unaccompanied by their families. Delimiting a residential area exclusively for "bachelors" is a project response for the great numbers of men attracted or recruited by a large-scale project. These workers typically participate in a migratory labor system, that is, the social reproduction of their families takes place in areas different from that where they work (Burawoy 1976).

The El Pinar camp is located ten kilometers from Ituzaingó and five kilometers from the construction site. Its location between the main residential areas for skilled workers and the construction site is indicative of the class bias that informs the planning of the settlement patterns of large-scale projects. This sizable population of male workers is viewed as potentially dangerous for the families of the other people in the area. First, a large population of unskilled labor workers is recruited without the possibility of bringing their families. Then these men are concentrated in labor camps that are clearly separated from the other residential areas where skilled workers and professionals live with their families.

The rationale underlying the concentration of unskilled workers in camps is a combination of least-cost solution reasoning with social and generational preconceptions influenced by class, generational, and gender-oriented biases. It is clear that the costs for housing projects compatible with family life are much higher than the construction of dormitories for bachelors.

The existence of a separate camp for "single" administrative personnel, the G2 camp, points to the need to consider more closely the importance of class-biased preconceptions in the segregation of male workers. The G2 camp is composed of twenty-one dormitories with a total of 296 places. It has its own restaurant and leisure facilities. By June 1986 there were 140 persons living in this area. Besides being a much smaller camp, there are other meaningful differences between G2 and El Pinar. Apart from the expected fact that the facilities in the G2 camp are better, many single women, part of ERIDAY's administrative staff, also live in G2. Furthermore, in contrast to El Pinar, G2 is located close to the pueblo of Ituzaingó. The rationale seems to be that although men clustered together in large numbers are always potentially dangerous (thus the creation of singles' areas), it is more likely to be so if in addition to being men, they are also workers. Thus, the workers' camps are located in areas distant from residential areas for families. In the end, the class line is more a determining factor than marital status.

The possibility of having access to a house seems to be the result of a complex combination of class and generational preconceptions. These preconceptions are related to the different positions in the labor market hierarchy as well as to the amount of access to power positions within the project as a whole.

Civil construction is a male industrial activity with one important particularity: the production process is mounted and discontinued every time a new job is begun. It is not an industrial activity where fixed capital is installed and permanently attached to a determinate location, such as a factory. Moving the production process from one place to another is a common routine in the construction branch of the economy. This creates specificities in terms of the necessary "immobilization of the labor force" (see my discussion of this notion in chapter 5). Barracks for workers are a common solution found in construction sites including those in urban situations. In a large-scale project this solution is magnified.

El Pinar is surrounded by a barbed-wire fence and its entrance is permanently guarded by the Argentine National Guard. The fence and the constant presence of the military imparts the immediate character of a total institution to this housing area. Indeed, some people call it "Alcatraz." Workers have to conform to the organization of spatial and temporal patterns intimately related to the needs of the organizers of production. The absence of families in the labor camp destroys the possibility of having household private space. Private space is conditioned by the work sphere to a much larger degree than in the Villa Permanente. Workers are managed through different collective daily experiences such as daily meals in the mess hall and going to and coming from the construction site. The project has a transportation system that includes a fleet of buses to transport workers to and from their residential quarters.

The concentration of men in a housing project for singles raises particularities that are often dealt with as a security problem. One problem involves the sexual lives of these men who are isolated from daily interaction with women. The development of large-scale prostitution is a characteristic of large-scale projects in general, a reflection of the skewed demographics created by the kind of labor market and migratory flows associated with these projects (Ribeiro 1987). In Yacyretá men cross the construction site area and go to the cheaper Paraguayan brothels. There has also been traffic of Paraguayan prostitutes to the area of El Pinar; these prostitutes may stay for longer periods of time. Homosexuality is also common in the El Pinar camp.

As a crude reflection of class relationships, the El Pinar indicates that in the formation of the labor force the unskilled segment of the labor market tends to be conceived as a potential source of social conflicts. At the same time, the conditions created by the project to govern the daily lives of these men stimulate their potential for social conflict. Days filled with back-breaking work, conflicts in the labor relations, spatial and social isolation, the skewed demographic composition, and the "total institution" character of the labor camp are some of the project-related factors that shape the social experience of this segment of the labor force.

# 5  Dividing the World: The Dynamics of Yacyretá's Labor Market Segmentation

The analysis of the labor market for a large-scale project is particularly valuable because the labor market is a central component of an entirely planned process. Labor market planning is a sophisticated task performed and controlled by highly specialized professionals, such as senior engineers and business administrators with graduate degrees. The timetable is carefully designed to respond to different project needs over a long-term cycle of production, a cycle that is susceptible to several kinds of fluctuations and variances, such as lack of adequate financing or political changes.

Assuming a perfect disturbance-free world, the planning of the labor market is a combination of different variables related to logistical needs—for example, the what, when, and how of equipment, material, and manpower, and the technical requirements of overlapping, sequential production phases. The peak of the complexity of the arrangements coincides with the peak of the growth of the labor force. It occurs when the construction work overlaps with the arrival of the electromechanical equipment and the beginning of its installation within the dam. This period represents the most complex combination of production activities with the greatest internal differentiation of a hydroelectric dam's labor force.

The differentiation of the labor market is frequently represented by means of graphs where the main variables are time and various technical and professional needs; a large-scale project is a set of multiple tasks with numerous deadlines to be accomplished. The total labor force of a project is depicted in terms of an imaginary curve representing the optimum growth of the labor force. This curve is used as a parameter to maintain control of the ideal and real growths of the labor force in relationship to the scheduling of the project as a whole. Labor managers keep track of the growth of the labor force and issue reports that are part of monthly assessments of the state of the project.

Similarly to what occurs with other planned actions, there is a difference between what is initially conceived and what becomes reality. The planning of Yacyretá's labor market could not have been immune to the changes of the Argentine economy which, in turn, also reflect changes in the world economy. In the mid-1980s, in view of the Argentine economic crisis and the lack of access to international financial sources caused by the indebtedness of the Argentine state, the scheduling for the project underwent deep restructuring. The 1990 deadline for the start of the operations of the first turbine became 1992. The peak of the main contractor's labor force (9,250 men) that was supposed to occur in 1987 was reestimated and reduced by one-third of the initial assumption. The difference between the planning of the labor force and the process through which it is created must be confronted frequently by labor managers.

Any project has its own labor needs. They are defined in a variety of ways related to the multiple activities that have to be carried out in the erection of a complex structure such as a huge hydroelectric dam. The numerous labor needs of a project cannot be entirely fullfilled by either local or regional populations. People have to be brought to the construction site from diverse points within the national territory or from abroad, to fill different types of positions within the labor structure.

Civil engineering is a highly hierarchical industrial activity. On one hand, in civil engineering there are clearly defined unskilled labor positions, that is, positions in which workers are at the lowest hierarchical levels and who basically move objects and respond to commands to perform simple operations. This is particularly evident in countries, such as those in Latin America, where construction is a labor-intensive activity. In these cases, unskilled positions are often occupied by recently proletarianized men, former peasants or cowboys, for instance. On the other hand, in civil engineering there are positions for sophisticated technicians and professionals, such as engineers, architects, and geologists.

Upward mobility within the system is frequent, including among workers, since it is common to learn new skills in the workplace. This process, highly marked by a hierarchical system, is heavily dependent on personal relationships with social actors who occupy higher positions. Patron-client relationships exist, but this situation cannot be purely characterized in terms of clientelism. To do so would underplay the need for mutual predictability and trust that is part of the work situation in engineering.

There is a limit to this upward mobility, however; it is restricted by a lack of a formal education. Despite a worker's knowledge, he cannot cross the line that separates engineers and other professionals—the controllers of the production process—from technicians and skilled workers. This does not mean, however, that personal relationships and practical knowledge on the job cease to be important. Foremen that have begun their careers as rank-and-file workers can play important advisory and mediating roles between managers and skilled workers. In Yacyretá, for instance, foremen who had participated in the construction of several dams worldwide in the last thirty years were highly valued by engineers for the practical knowledge they had at their command.

In a large-scale project such as Yacyretá, the segmentation of the labor market is defined by the internal hierarchical organization of the labor division as well as by other factors associated with the processes of formation of large-scale projects' labor forces. In fact, there are several labor flows structuring the formation of these labor forces. Different positions in the labor market are associated with different migratory phenomena. Before discussing the intricate relationships among positions within a labor market and migratory flows, it is necessary to introduce a notion of labor market segmentation that goes beyond the internal hierarchical logic and division of labor of civil engineering as an industrial branch.

Labor market segmentation is a notion that is useful to interpret broad units of analysis (such as a certain nation-state labor-market) or more concrete and situated units such as a unit of production (e.g., a plantation, a factory, or a large-scale project). This notion has been developed by authors discussing varying degrees of access to the labor market. It has been especially marked by the analysis of sociological contexts where racial or ethnic factors are crucial to understand positions in the labor market (Gordon 1972; Bonacich 1972). This conception has been introduced into the body of anthropological literature. Eric

Wolf (1982, 379–81), elaborating on previous discussions, stresses the ethnic underpinning of the formation of labor markets worldwide. He is interested in the "juxtaposition of groups of different social and cultural origins."

Wolf discusses the "ethnic segmentation of the labor market" in relationship to the historical process of capitalist expansion: "Social and cultural heterogeneity . . . must itself be located in the organization of the labor process. The diverse groups brought together did, of course, make use of distinctive cultural forms to build ties of kinship, friendship, religious affiliation, common interest, and political association in order to maximize access to resources in competition with one another. Such activity, however, cannot be understood without seeing it in relation to the ways different cohorts of the working class were brought into the process of capitalist accumulation" (Wolf 1982, 379).

Yacyretá's labor market is ethnically segmented because several populations with diverse social and cultural backgrounds are put together by the project. But a further distinction needs to be drawn in relation to Yacyretá. Within the Argentine segment of the labor force, for instance, the segmentation is marked by different regional origins; that is, there are different groups of workers that come from different provinces and regions of Argentina.

I am not going to consider the formation and dynamics of the labor market related to the period of construction of the infrastructure of the project, when the domination of the construction process by Argentine contractors implied a simpler labor market structuring. I will focus instead on Yacyretá's labor market when the main civil work contract, the core of this large-scale project, began to be executed. In fact, the coming of ERIDAY to Ituzaingó in early 1984 meant the beginning of the full unfolding of the complexity of Yacyretá's labor market.

### The Labor Market Segmentation of the Yacyretá Project

In a project's institutional triangle, the main contractor is the principal actor in terms of labor relations. Consequently, ERIDAY's labor force is the largest and most representative of the complexity of Yacyretá's labor market and will be the basis of my analysis.

The ethnic segmentation of the labor market stands out in the construction of Yacyretá: there are thousands of Paraguayans and Argentines working together under the direction of European managers (see fig. 5). Each of these segments of the labor force has specific legal labor relations with its employer, ERIDAY. These relations are classified in terms of three different labor contracts: Argentine, Paraguayan, and European labor contracts. The consideration of Yacyretá's labor market ethnic segmentation is important not only for its demographic and cultural implications, but also because it is directly related to different types of labor relations.

### The Argentine-Paraguayan Dividing Line

The first line cutting across Yacyretá's labor market splits it into two large segments, one Paraguayan and one Argentine. In February 1986, for instance, ERIDAY employed 1,808 bearers of Argentine contracts and 1,448 of Paraguayan contracts. The Argentine-Paraguayan division was defined in the beginning of the formal existence of the project by the Yacyretá Treaty signed by the two governments in December 1973. This legal obligation generated interesting sociological, juridical, and anthropological questions. It is a labor market that is split by necessity in terms of nationalities. There are, thus, two working classes with different historical, political, and cultural backgrounds working for the same employer, ERIDAY. Labor/capital relationships are regulated by distinct bodies of labor legislation that ultimately reflect the different levels of development of the Paraguayan and Argentine production forces and the histories of class relations in each country.

Given Argentina's relatively higher industrial development, the local working class is sizable. The Argentine working class has a powerful tradition of unionism, one that makes it a necessary interlocutor—via CGT, Confederación General del Trabajo (General Confederation of Labor)—in the country's political and economic life. The political and mobilization power of the unions is an every day fact in Argentina. One of the largest unions in the country is UOCRA, Unión de los Trabajadores de la Construcción Civil de la República Argentina (Union of the Workers in the Civil Construction of the Argentine Republic). The fact that Yacyretá is the largest concentration of civil construction workers in Argentina makes the local Ituzaingó-based union visible on the national scene. The history of the local UOCRA reflects a permanent conflict between grass-roots unionists and UOCRA's leadership at the regional and national levels. The latter is often

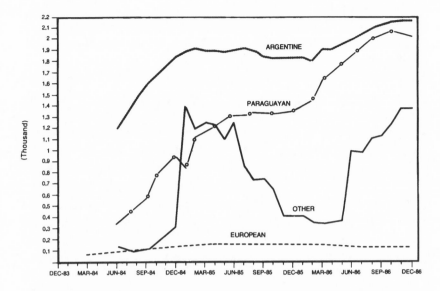

Figure 5. Growth of contractor's work force (by type of contract). *Source:* company records.

seen as having become a bureaucracy primarily interested in its internal power dynamics and its relationships to other important national political actors. The ideological spectrum of the Ituzaingó-UOCRA ranged from the Peronist Right to the Peronist Left, with a parallel and sizable influence from the Marxist-Leninist parties, especially the PCA, the Argentine Communist Party (see *Qué Pasa?*, the official PCA newspaper, of October 1986).

Yacyretá labor managers are aware that they are dealing with highly politicized union leaders who are capable of stopping the construction work in search of better socioeconomic rewards, or in response to CGT's calls for national strikes to protest national economic policy.

Paraguay's national economy has been structured basically around agricultural production and contraband to Brazil and Argentina. Nevertheless, the construction of the Paraguayan-Brazilian Itaipú hydroelectric dam (1975–82) represented a shift in the country's socioeconomic profile. The completion of this dam meant the end of a bonanza period in which U.S.$1 billion entered Paraguay. In this period, a developmental illusion flourished, stimulating the belief that economic growth was steady and irreversible. The completion of Itaipú also generated a recession composed of three main factors: the stop of the flow of hard currencies associated with the Itaipú project; the lay-off of thousands of recently proletarianized workers; and the idle-capacity of the Paraguayan contractors, a sensitive issue in the post-Itaipú era because after agriculture, construction is the second most important economic activity in terms of generating employment.

Indeed, half of Itaipú's total labor force of 40,000 men came from Paraguay. Paraguayan firms intended to transfer equipment and manpower from Itaipú to Yacyretá in order to counterbalance the recessive effects of Itaipú's completion. This finally happened, but with an important peculiarity: the completion of Itaipú's main civil works did not coincide with the mobilization of Yacyretá's main contractor of which CONEMPA, a major Paraguayan contractor that had participated in Itaipú's construction, was a member. Furthermore, given the Argentine economic crisis, Yacyretá was never launched with the intensity expected in Paraguay (*Hoy,* Asunción, September 13, 1985).

In contrast to Argentina, Paraguay did not have a working class with an industrial labor past or with political importance in national affairs. On the contrary, in a country dominated from 1954 to 1989 by a conservative authoritarian government, the prospect of developing a unionized and politically active working class was a probable outcome of the country's participation in two major construction projects, Itaipú and Yacyretá, and was not exactly welcome. Additionally, Paraguayan officials feared that the workers' contact with a working class that was conscious of its political importance, such as the Argentine one, would produce undesirable side-effects on Paraguayan class relations in the long run. In daily contact at the work site, Paraguayan workers would get acquainted with the power of Argentine unions and with the comparatively more advanced Argentine labor legislation, as indeed they did.

The inherent contradictions of bringing together two working classes were first dealt with in juridical terms. Argentina and Paraguay have labor and social security laws that reflect the histories of these nations and the negotiating power of their working classes. Citizens from both countries would be working in a binational area, Yacyretá's construction site, and, mostly, for the same employer, ERIDAY. A new arrangement to deal with this reality was necessary. The legal solution was a hybrid piece of international law called the Protocolo de Trabajo y Seguridad Social (Labor and Social Security Protocol). A sort of internal labor legislation of the Yacyretá project, it was supposed to supersede the Paraguayan and Argentine legislations (EBY 1986, 189–98). Juridical ambiguity, typical of large-scale projects, was translated into a formal legislation that proved to be ambiguous in itself. To work in the Yacyretá project does not mean that national labor legislations automatically cease to protect a person from his or her employers. The importance of citizenship rights is reflected in the legal relationships ERIDAY maintains with its personnel. There is a basic distinction between people hired on the Paraguayan side or on the Argentine side of the project. A third category, much smaller but very powerful because of the position its members occupy, is formed by people that have "European contracts."

The ambiguity of the legal framework has been a constant source of conflicts in the area. In general terms, the Protocolo tends to be more advanced than Paraguayan legislation and less so than Argentine law. Yacyretá's workers manipulate two bodies of legislation; that is, their respective national legislations and the binational labor legislation, the Protocolo.

Evidently, workers are not the only ones to manipulate the effects of the Argentine-Paraguayan segmentation. Managers do also. To constantly consider the different social reproduction costs of the two working classes is a well-known form of manipulating labor market segmentation. Argentine workers have access to better welfare systems and are used to higher social standards of living than Paraguayan workers. At the same time, Argentine economic reality makes living more expensive in that country compared with Paraguay. Paraguayans receive smaller wages when compared to Argentines in a hard currency. This is an important consideration for economic actors who operate at the level of the world-system, especially because the book-keeping currency of the project is the U.S. dollar.

Managers may manipulate the binationality of the labor force by hiring different numbers of Paraguayan and Argentine workers according to various technical segments of the project. For instance, in Yacyretá, given the technical characteristics of the job, earth movement is an important activity performed by skilled workers. Argentine union leaders were increasingly disconcerted with what they understood as a propensity of managers to hire Paraguayan personnel for the earth movement sector. Managers' reasons were not exclusively based on economic factors, such as wages, but were also based on political factors. Earth movement

Argentine workers are a segment of the civil construction union that is especially active in the local labor movement. Argentine union leaders also disliked the fact that a sizable number of Uruguayans, who have been working for the main contractor's leading firm since the construction of the Uruguayan-Argentine Salto Grande Dam, occupied powerful positions within ERIDAY.

Knowledge of how to relate to the local working class, in other words, to have a grasp of its political history and cultural characteristics, is an asset for managers directly involved with labor relations. Some of the firms of Yacyretá's main contractor, including the European ones, have a long-standing knowledge of Argentine large-scale project workers. Most of the managers I interviewed within ERIDAY and EBY displayed a knowledge about the Argentine working class that, although marked by class and sometimes ethnic biases, included references to technical, cultural, political, and ideological differences.

ERIDAY also relies on the experience of a Paraguayan firm, CONEMPA, an important contractor in Itaipú's construction. Actually, the transference of men from one construction site to another is an essential characteristic of the labor markets for large-scale projects. This migration creates long-standing social networks that maintain a cohesiveness by participating in other large-scale projects. Before discussing the importance of this characteristic of the labor markets for large-scale projects, a word must be said on the internal segmentation of the Argentine working class.

### The Regional Segmentation of the Argentine Labor Force

For the purposes of my analysis the following expressions will have these meanings attached to them: (a) *local-level population* will mean the population of the Argentine Department of Ituzaingó and other adjacent departments of the province of Corrientes; (b) *regional-level population* will include the population of the departments of the province of Corrientes located far from the construction site, and the other provinces forming the Argentine Northeast (Misiones, Chaco, and Formosa); (c) *national-level population* will mean the population of all Argentine provinces but the ones previously mentioned.

According to the February 1986 Argentine paylist, foreigners—Uruguayans (the largest group), Paraguayans, Bolivians, and one Italian—

accounted for only 3.5 percent of a total of 1,808 bearers of Argentine labor contracts. The following analysis is based on data from this document and from newly generated information on Yacyretá's labor market that was given to me in Ituzaingó both by EBY and ERIDAY.

The main contractor's personnel hired on the Argentine side of the project is segmented by provincial origin (see fig. 6). Although these people come from all Argentine provinces, the different weight of the provincial origins seems to correlate with factors stemming from the logistics and migratory circuits of large-scale projects in Argentina rather than with geographical proximity or the power of attraction that the project may represent to migrant labor.

Almost 70 percent of a total 1,808 Argentines had come, in February 1986, from four provinces: Corrientes (40.5 percent), Entre Ríos (17.5 percent), Neuquén (6.0 percent) and Misiones (5.2 percent). This distribution allows us to think about the relationship between the formation of Yacyretá's labor market, Yacyretá's power to attract labor, and the labor flows associated with large-scale projects within Argentina.

First, the numbers clearly show that the province of Corrientes, where the project is located, supplies by far the largest number of men to the labor market. According to data elaborated by the main contractor at my request, in June 1986 approximately half of the Correntino segment of the Argentine labor force had come from the department of Ituzaingó itself. The Ituzaingueños, though, typically occupied the unskilled segment of the labor market (86.3 percent out of a total of 395 workers).

Before the advent of the Yacyretá project in the area, the pueblo of Ituzaingó was the head of a department where most of the local labor force was engaged in activities connected with agriculture and cattle ranching. The project caused a shift from agricultural activities, involving mixed relations of production typical of populations undergoing processes of proletarianization, to full wage-labor relations. This population filled the most subordinate positions within the project's labor market. Perceiving with insight that his structural position had not changed with the presence of the project, a local cowboy, a gaucho currently working in Yacyretá said: "for me ERIDAY is just another estancia" (cattle ranch). Nevertheless, because of the possibilities for upward mobility typical of civil engineering labor markets, it is likely that some individuals from Ituzaingó will learn new skills and reach positions of skilled workers.

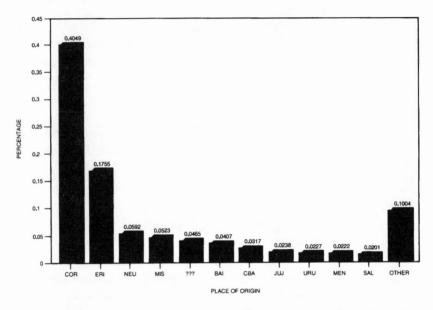

Figure 6. Origin of Argentine labor force. COR, Corrientes; ERI, Entre Ríos; NEU, Neuquén; MIS, Misiones; BAI, Buenos Aires; CBA, Córdoba; JUJ, Jujuy; URU, Uruguay; MEN, Mendoza; SAL, Salta.

Yacyretá also meant a strong demand for services in the area. Some services, such as the daily cleaning of offices and domestic services for the elite of the project, are performed mostly by local women.

The fact that the province of Corrientes contributed the largest number of workers to the formation of the Argentine segment of Yacyretá could lead one to overemphasize location, and proximity to the site of the project as the main factors underlying the creation and internal differentiation of the Argentine segment of the labor market. If this were the case, we could expect to have a large segment of regional population participating at the project. This does not occur, however. In February 1986, for instance, people coming from the other provinces of the northeast region accounted for only 7.7 percent. Neighboring Misiones—a province that has historically been influential in the economic life of the Ituzaingó area due to the proximity of its capital, Posadas—contributed to the work force only 5.2 percent of the participating regional population. Chaco and Formosa contributed with only 1.7 percent and 0.7 percent, respectively.

Among the four largest contributors to the formation of the Argentine labor force, and ahead of Misiones, were the provinces of Entre Ríos and Neuquén with 17.5 and 6.0 percent, respectively. The argument that the project's proximity is the prime factor would explain the significant number of workers from Entre Ríos. In fact, Corrientes's southern border is with the province of Entre Ríos. But, what would explain the fact that Neuquén, a province located in the south of Argentina and more than 1,000 miles from Corrientes, is the third largest source of labor, ahead of neighboring Misiones?

The answer is easier than the formulation of the question. Entre Ríos was the site of the construction of a major project, the Salto Grande Argentine-Uruguayan hydroelectric dam, in which Impregilo, the lead firm of Yacyretá's main contractor, has also participated. By the same token, Neuquén is a province where several main Argentine hydroelectric dams have been built in the last decades by Impregilo. In fact, this contractor was building another dam in Neuquén, Piedra del Aguila. It may be concluded, therefore, that the different weights of the main provincial segments of the Argentine labor market are heavily influenced by the transference of manpower by contractors from previous work sites to Yacyretá. In this connection, Yacyretá's labor market is structured more by the action of contractors than by spontaneous factors such as a project's power to attract or its physical proximity.

The following are the different large-scale projects from where almost 30 percent (as of June 15, 1986) of ERIDAY's total work force (bearers of Argentine, Paraguayan, and European contracts) came to Yacyretá. They are, in order of importance, (1) Salto Grande (Entre Ríos), (2) Itaipú Binacional (Brazil/Paraguay), (3) Alicurá (Neuquén), (4) Planicie Banderita (Neuquén), and (5) Acaray Central Hidroeléctrica (Hernandarias, Paraguay). The sixth position is formed by the following set of projects: Casa de Piedra (Río Negro), Central Atómica Embalse Río Tercero (Córdoba), El Chocón (Neuquén), Carrisal (Mendoza), and Valle Grande (Mendoza).

The transfer of people from one large-scale project to another on a national scale generates an important migratory movement. When unskilled labor is available at the local level, a contractor can hire local people to fill unskilled positions. This is why the participation of Correntinos is so prominent. The higher in the hierarchy of technical and professional qualification, the more likely it is that the contractor will transfer its personnel from previous jobs, be they completed or still in execution.

The continuous transference of manpower from one project to another is a phenomenon I call the large-scale project migratory circuit. Although a substantial part of the Argentine labor force participates in this circuit—54.2 percent as of June 15, 1986—I will describe the circuit's internal characteristics after a discussion on the European segment of Yacyretá's labor market that best illustrates this phenomenon.

Let me point briefly to some of the effects of the project's regional segmentation on the social life of ERIDAY's employees. The 1,000 Viviendas, the residential area of ERIDAY's skilled personnel, is intensely marked by regional segmentation. Although there are major blocks of people from particular provinces, there is such diversity of regional origins that several of the 1,000 Viviendas dwellers commented that they were now able to see and experience a cultural diversity that they thought did not exist in Argentina.

Besides allowing for positive experiences of cultural diversity, regional segmentation also created problems, such as the heterogeneous educational background of the children studying at the 1,000 Viviendas Argentine school. Integration among Argentines is also an issue that is most often dealt with through the manifestation of cultural markers such as food preparation, different styles of *mate* drinking, and music. A music festival organized in 1986, under the initiative of the Ituzainguenos and sponsored by EBY and ERIDAY, was intended to "cement" the mosaic of regional and national cultures. According to one of its organizers, music was thought of as the best way to integrate people. He said: "If you don't like music, you don't like anything."

### The Expatriate European Segment

Expatriates are a common presence in large-scale projects worldwide (Murphy 1983, 32). In fact, the labor market of the expatriate is the world market. In this sense, they can be thought of as inhabitants of the world-system, or better, as inhabitants of the small villages of the world-system. Their importance in terms of the size of their group varies according to a project's location and complexity. Thus, when a project is developed in a country where the local labor force has little experience in large-scale contruction works, the number of expatriates tends to increase. According to some of the managers at Yacyretá, the less industrialized the country, the larger the expatriate segment of the work force tends to be. Consequently, in some cases, transnational corporations may transfer to work sites not only the typical components of the expatriate segment (professionals, highly skilled technicians, and administrative personnel), but also unskilled workers.

The internal composition of the European segment of Yacyretá's labor market replicates the arrangement among several European contractors that formalized the creation of ERIDAY, a subject discussed in chapter 2 of this book. Italians represent the largest population of foreigners in the Yacyretá project, followed by French. The growth of the total number of holders of European labor contracts working in the construction site is shown in figure 7. Their importance in the project stems not from their numbers but from the fact that they form a closed managerial power elite. On February 28, 1986, for instance, there were 140 Europeans living in Yacyretá, less than 4 percent of ERIDAY's labor force. Their nationalities were Italian, 83; French, 45; German, 10; and Austrian, 2.

Italians and French accounted for 91.4 percent of the total number. In Yacyretá, Italians are relatively more powerful than French, another fact reflecting the negotiations and formalization of ERIDAY's existence. It is not only because of varying degrees of access to managerial power that ethnicity is an issue among these managers. Indeed, ethnic identities always arise in a contrastive context. Italian and French managers I interviewed also perceived each other in terms of their nationalities and what that meant for the daily administration of the project. Italian managers, for instance, think of themselves as more pragmatic, less bureaucratic, and more site-oriented people, professionals who can make decisions on site without engaging in further studies in the office. They often talk about their personnel in the construction site as if they were a family. On the other hand, Frenchmen see themselves as more acquainted with modern corporate ideas, with an impersonal conception of management. Both Italians and French tend to blame each other for daily administrative problems. They seldom socialize together. In fact, Italians, French, and Germans tend to form separate closed groups.

Since the Italians represented the largest and most powerful segment of the European population at Yacycretá, I focused my attention on them. But most of what follows could be applied to other foreigners, including those working for CIDY, the consultant.

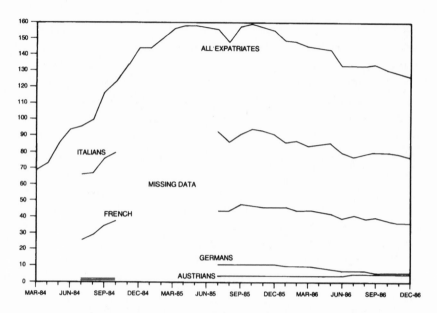

Figure 7. Country of origin of principal expatriate groups. *Source:* company records.

ERIDAY's Italian personnel has been transferred by Impregilo from several large-scale projects, most of them located in Argentina and other Latin American countries. I believe international contractors tend to transfer their personnel within the same world region not only because of cost efficiency, but also because knowledge of the local language is a valuable asset at the work site. In June 1986, out of eighty-six Italians working in Yacyretá, seventy-seven (89.5 percent) had previously participated in at least one project. Reflecting Impregilo's long-standing presence in the Argentine market, fifty-two people had come from the Salto Grande (17) and Alicurá (35) projects in Argentina. A group of ten had come from Pakistan, and the remaining fifteen had previously worked in construction projects in Peru, Ecuador, Colombia, Panamá, Venezuela, and Itaipú (Brazil-Paraguay).

The Italians working for ERIDAY are bearers of "European labor contracts," a category that entitles them to a set of fringe benefits. The distinctive treatment to which the European personnel are privy is visible within ERIDAY's administrative structure. There is a separate department of personnel that deals with the specific questions of the European staff. Some of the benefits most Italians have, such as having a car permanently available, stem from the high positions they occupy within the labor market hierarchy rather than from the fact that they are Europeans. Nevertheless, they are entitled to services that are directly related to their conditions of expatriates, such as periodic trips to their home country, accommodations in first-class hotels in Buenos Aires on their ways to or from Italy, access to health care in international centers, access to Italian videotapes, magazines and newspapers, and a more generous treatment from the powerful Servicios Generales (General Services), ERIDAY's administrative unit that takes care of community life.

Technicians and professionals experienced in large-scale projects are a valuable asset for transnational corporations. Managers want to keep the skilled segment of the labor market from leaving their jobs. Expatriates who have worked in different countries under different working conditions are considered highly in the market. The provision of adequate services is one of the measures through which managers keep the expatriate segment within a large-scale project labor market. Despite the fact that fringe benefits, such as free housing in projects' residential areas, are an important consideration, expatriates are primarily attracted to large-scale projects by immediate comparative economic advantages represented by higher wages. In Yacyretá, an Italian technician, for instance, may earn three times more than in his home country. Furthermore, expatriates receive an extra payment—the carovita, or "pocket money"—intended to cover their local expenses. In Yacyretá some of my informants thought the amount of the "pocket money" paid was not sufficient, forcing them to use part of their regular wages.

Nevertheless, expatriates could save either their entire wages or a substantial part of it, making investments back in their home country. Saving is possible not only because of the fringe benefits and higher wages, but also because living in a work-site community reduces the general cost of living of this segment of the labor force. Expatriates cannot have full access and exposure to the sophisticated markets and consumption patterns of their home countries in these isolated areas. Indeed, as one of them told me, "living in Ituzaingó makes me feel like a peasant when I go to Posadas [the capital of Misiones and largest city close to Yacyretá] and see all those stores."

Although it is true that becoming an expatriate is a condition into which individuals enter for economic reasons, their reasons for remaining cannot be entirely reduced to individual economic calculations. Managers are increasingly aware that the large-scale project environment is conducive to several types of social conflicts due to the specificities of life around a work site. They, therefore, foster a sense of community among the labor force as part of the internal managerial rationale to develop a large-scale project. Kathleen Murphy in her book directed to assist managers involved in large-scale projects' administration states the following: "The expatriates—or 'expats,' as they frequently call themselves—are out of their element, living on the fringes of a strange environment. The conditions are tough; the climate is often hot; tropical diseases are common. Medical problems are intensified, due to a shortage of doctors and hospitals. . . . As is common in most 'marginal' situations, social unrest is widespread, leading to alcoholism, divorce, boredom, supermarket complaints, fistfights, and sometimes even murder. Thus, the project manager must somehow create a sense of community among these expats to diminish the sense of social isolation" (Murphy 1983, 32). She also considers that creating a sense of community is a way to minimize turnover (ibid., 166).

In reality, expatriates do enter large-scale project markets for economic reasons, but they remain within it for several reasons. In order to understand the range of factors involved in this question we need to consider the existence and dynamics of what I call the large-scale project migratory circuit and the creation of the so-called bicho-de-obra identity.

### The Large-Scale Project Migratory Circuit and the Creation of the "Bicho-de-Obra" Identity

The owners of industrial capital need to establish stable labor forces because industrial activities demand a predictable number of workers on a daily basis. A way of confronting overcosts caused by turnover is through what José Sérgio Leite Lopes (1979) calls the immobilization of the labor force through housing. Leite Lopes did a historical and anthropological analysis of the development of what he calls the "complex factory-with-labor-quarters" in a textile industry in the northeast of Brazil. He showed how from an initial need to immobilize a labor force recently proletarianized, this complex grew to become a city. He was also concerned with the interference of the dynamics and interests of the industrial production logic in workers' private lives through the manipulation of the factory's housing quarters, by management. For Leite Lopes, "the fact that some industries provide housing to their workers, in return for either a rent deducted from the wages or for economic or noneconomic obligations that were not explicit in the labor contract but incorporated to the behavior of workers as part of the rules of the game, implies a direct and visible interference . . . of the factory's management in workers' individual consumptions" (Leite Lopes 1979, 42).

This situation is accompanied by specificities in the relations between labor and capital such as an invasion by the production domain into "extra-labor relations domains," like housing and daily life outside the factory. Workers' quarters are conceived as a way of concentrating a great number of people that become dependent upon management not only through wages but also through housing. Furthermore, housing is also seen as an effective way to maintain a population to be constantly present and available for production ends. It also facilitates the political control of workers because quarters may be used as another element of pressure and negotiation.

Following Karl Marx's (1977, 818–22) indications of the existence of a "nomad proletariat," typical of large-scale construction projects such as railroads, Leite Lopes estimates that such a work force can be considered nomad only when connected with a sequence of employments. *Nomadism* would refer, thus, to the sequential movements from one employment to another. But "within each job experience the 'nomad proletariat' is immobilized through housing in the sense that the employer controls other spheres of a worker's life beyond the work relationship. . . . this control would be even greater in the case of the 'nomad proletariat' in comparison to a stable work force" (Leite Lopes 1979, 46).

Spatial mobility is a central specificity of the engineering industry, since the mobility of investments induces the rotation of the labor force (Panaia 1985, 11ff.). Migrant labor is thus directly associated with this industrial branch. This is especially evident when construction is being done in isolated areas. Every time a new job begins in isolated areas, contractors have to transfer manpower and equipment to the new work site.

The formation of a labor market for a large-scale project entails several migratory movements and associated social changes. It is true that what could be called *industrial nomadism* is a condition that affects workers, but it is not exclusive to them. I will focus on the segment of Yacyretá's labor market that most fully lives within the limits of a closed migratory circuit:

skilled workers, technicians, and professionals. Before moving ahead to this discussion, though, I will present other migratory-related social changes associated with large-scale projects.

When a large-scale project is under way, the local population is almost always forced to resettle or to become proletarians engaged in the lower levels of the project's labor market. Regional and sometimes national populations may also be recruited through what I call *organized labor flows*. This term supposes

> the existence of a structure, normally provided by the state, that controls access to the territory of a large-scale project. Several agencies, or most likely one large agency, *recruit, select,* and *send* workers to the area, thus assuming brokerage functions. By deliberately controlling recruitment, selection, and access to the area, these agencies define the general profile of the labor force that is to be engaged in a large-scale project: male, young, and healthy workers unaccompanied by their families. The organized flow prevents demographic pressures on the territory by people not directly useful to the project—old and unhealthy men and women and children. (Ribeiro 1987, 14)

In these circumstances, the relationships between migration, the labor needs of the projects, and the effects on the sociodemographic structure of the created population are transparent.

The experience of a significant part of large-scale project workers, approximates what Michael Burawoy (1976) defines as "migratory labor systems." A central characteristic of these systems is the geographical separation between the location of the workplace and the region where the social reproduction of workers' families occurs. In situations such as those described by Burawoy for migrant mine workers in South Africa and migrant farm workers in the United States, labor contractors take advantage of the different costs of the social reproduction of the workers' labor force. According to Burawoy, "one consequence of a system of migrant labor is the externalization, to an alternate economy and/or state, of certain costs of labor-force renewal—costs normally borne by the employer and/or state of employment" (1976, 1,050). In this sense, the unskilled segment of large-scale projects can be thought of as participating in "migratory labor systems." As was shown in chapter 4, the housing area prepared for unskilled workers, the labor camps, has no space for family life.

In contrast to the unskilled segment of the labor market, most of the skilled workers, technicians, professionals, and part of the administrative personnel have access to family life at project sites. Indeed, since managers are interested in keeping their specialized personnel, corporations provide the services needed for recreating the life-style needs of the skilled segment of the labor market. It is the value placed on this segment of the labor market that makes it the archetypical component of large-scale projects' migratory circuits.

## The Large-Scale Project Migratory Circuit

Corporations that operate in large-scale project markets develop several works both in a given moment and over time. The simultaneous maintenance of several construction jobs is as important as a sequence of projects. Firms need new projects to sustain their economic viability over time and to ensure increasing returns of capital. Assignments need to be completed not only for projects that are already under way (and that may be themselves in different stages of production with distinct labor needs), but also for new projects that have just been won through bidding processes. In this connection, depending on whether it is a corporation operating at the level of national or international markets, firms establish national or global circuits of large-scale projects. The operational and administrative control of these circuits is ultimately centralized in national or world headquarters of corporations. Corporations, thus, either transfer personnel that are already working within the system or recruit new people who may become migrant labor who follow their employers' investments.

Clearly, if every time a construction was completed a firm had to dismiss its entire labor force and equipment, it would not survive for long in the market. In reality, all firms are striving constantly to maximize both their fixed and variable capitals, either synchronically or diachronically. Large-scale projects form a system, composed of different units of varying sizes and complexities, that may grow or shrink. Maximization of both the simultaneity and sequence of works is thus a main consideration in order to maintain and enhance the profitability of this system, since manpower and equipment are constantly being transferred among its units.

Nevertheless, corporations do not always need to maintain all their work force by transferring it from one job to another. Unskilled labor, for instance, may be found at the local level. There is no immediate economic reason why unskilled workers should be transferred from one project to another if there is a sizable local population that can be recruited. In this case, it may prove to be more economic to dismiss the unskilled segment of the labor force every time a project is completed and reestablish it every time a new construction starts. That is not the case, however, with the skilled segment. The more qualified and experienced the worker, the more likely corporations will compete for his work. The more a corporation is able to keep its body of highly trained and experienced personnel, the less it will need to search for them in the labor market. Therefore, it is the movement of the skilled segment of the labor force that most clearly typifies the existence of migratory circuits internal to the market of large-scale projects.

The parallel between access to better social services and greater qualification indicates managements' awareness of the importance of providing their skilled personnel with the possibility of reproducing a more regular social life, a sense of community. In this connection, the possibility of reproducing family life at construction sites is part of the necessary measures that corporations need to provide to retain their skilled personnel. Besides the provision of family houses, the most important aspect of this reproduction to the skilled workers is the availability of education for their children.

The possibility of social reproduction within large-scale projects environments is the basis for the existence of large-scale projects' migratory circuit. It is also the main feature distinguishing it from other less-skilled forms of migrant labor.

Professionals and technicians who work on large-scale projects tend to become specialists in such undertakings, forming a relatively reduced pool of people who are frequently invited by public or private corporations to participate in different construction projects. At the same time, they are career-oriented persons.

In Yacyretá, personal relationships that developed over several previous working experiences were visible in the circle of Argentine engineers, geologists, and technicians working for EBY, the consultant (CIDY), or the main contractor (ERIDAY). Personal acquaintances become entangled with professional careers since knowing each other's professional capabilities may mean references for future jobs.

For these people, the labor market is not a totally abstract entity controlled by objective laws of supply and demand. The labor market is also structured by social networks wherein professional capability and prestige is an asset that sometimes cannot be separated from qualitative aspects of intersubjective interaction—such as personal admiration, friendship, and previsibility of actors' behaviors—and that are irreducible to economic determinations or calculations. The importance of social networks for labor migration has been clearly stated by Alejandro Portes and Robert L. Bach: "labor migration can . . . be conceptualized as a process of network building, which depends on and, in turn, reinforces social relationships across space" (1985, 10).

A typical trajectory of a senior Argentine engineer involved participation in the construction of five dams in a period of almost twenty years. Since his first assignment after completion of his university degree, each new job meant upward mobility in his career. In his case, as in those of almost all other professionals I interviewed, personal relationships were instrumental in moving from one assignment to another. Friends and colleagues either revealed new oportunities in the market or pointed at that person's capability for a new position. In Yacyretá, this engineer again met with colleagues and friends that had made the Argentine circuit of large-scale projects through itineraries that did not totally coincide with the one he had experienced.

Because Impregilo, the lead firm of Yacyretá's main contractor, for decades has had a central position in Argentina's public works, the El Chocón to Salto Grande to Alicurá to Yacyretá (dams that Impregilo constructed) migration is the most common trajectory among Yacyretá's personnel participating in large-scale projects migratory circuit. For this reason, I consider that trajectory as the clearest illustration of a national large-scale project migratory circuit related to Yacyretá.

But Yacyretá is also a world-system happening, which is why it is also part of an international circuit of large-scale projects. In reality the foreign segment of Yacyretá's labor market, more than any other, fully illustrates the existence of large-scale project migratory circuits. Both CIDY and ERIDAY, the two components of the project's institutional triangle that rely on foreign personnel, had professionals in Yacyretá coming from jobs executed in countries such as the Philippines, Iran, Pakistan, Nigeria, El Salvador, Brazil, Venezuela, Peru, Ecuador, and Panamá. The neutralization of expatriates' citizenships is a beneficial by-product for the corporations. Being "world-system citizens," expatriates lose their political capabilities of intervening in the organized labor movements or in the body politic of the countries where projects are being carried out.

A large-scale project articulates national and international migration through the intersection of national and international large-scale project migratory circuits. At this intersection, members of a national migratory circuit may be co-opted to participate in the international circuit. In Yacyretá, the visible presence of Uruguayans, the largest group of foreigners—126 persons in December 1986 out of a total labor force of 5,641—is certainly related more to Impregilo's previous presence in Salto Grande than to the proximity of that country to Yacyretá's work site. Although the likelihood that a participant of the international circuit would be co-opted by the national circuit is a small one, it is potentially real. Indeed, some of the Italians that have been working for Impregilo in Argentina for more than ten years considered the possibility of fixing residence in that country. At this level, personal reasons were influential, such as having formed a binational marriage or being in a stage of the developmental cycle of the domestic group where stability is prioritized to the detriment of mobility.

In contrast to the most common streams of labor migration, the large-scale project migrants most often find themselves in a more powerful position than the local population, since they tend to occupy the upper levels of the labor market. Contemporary discussions emphasize labor migration as occurring in a larger scenario structured by the uneven works of capitalist expansion. The analysis of large-scale project migratory circuits certainly corroborates conceptualizations, like the following one, that look at labor flows as internal to the same economic system. "Migration has a dual economic function: from the standpoint of capital, it is the means to fulfill labor demand at different points of the system; from the standpoint of labor, it is the means to take advantage of opportunities distributed unequally in space" (Portes and Bach 1985, 9).

The large-scale project migratory circuit can be considered as an example of occupational migration, that is, a migratory movement that is basically determined by the mobility of a person's occupation, with several implications for migrants. Its impact on family life is an important issue that needs further research. Many of my informants mentioned, for instance, what they considered to be an unusual number of divorces within Yacyretá's population.

Different occupational categories could be analyzed considering the migratory circuits they engender. An industrial activity that certainly generates a migratory circuit of its own is the oil industry (see Olien and Olien 1982). Parallels and analogies between the migratory circuits of large-scale projects and the transferences of military and diplomatic personnel could also be explored. But to further explain the complexity of the large-scale project migratory circuit I will focus on its typical inhabitant: the bicho-de-obra.

## Ambiguity and Permanence: The Bicho-de-Obra

Bicho-de-obra is an expression some Argentine participants in the large-scale project migratory circuit use to classify themselves. Its literal translation would be "construction-site insect." But considering the existence of some U.S. expressions such as "party animal," I will translate it as "work-site animal." I will use this label to mean the population that typically develops its work and social life within large-scale project migratory circuits. Since construction is almost exclusively a male occupation I will consider the typical bicho-de-obra as being a man. That does not mean that there are no women participating in the large-scale project migratory circuit. Women in the circuit most typically are present as relatives (wives and daughters) of employed men. Some of these women may be hired by the project to do administrative work or to teach at one of the project's schools.

My attention was first directed toward the importance of the existence of the bicho-de-obra when I noticed that a sizable part of Yacyretá's population had previously participated in other projects. I then began to investigate when, why, and how people entered the large-scale project migratory circuit. But the question why many of them never seemed to leave the circuit soon became more important than all others. Although it was clear that people entered the circuit because of professional reasons—such as career requirements proper to engineering, geology, and other technical occupations of the construction industry—or because of economic calculations aimed at taking advantage of fringe benefits due to jobs' hardships; they also remained within the circuit despite the fact that their economic objectives were fulfilled.

I began to consider, then, that the participants of large-scale project migratory circuits formed a discrete social category, defined basically by the dynamics of its work life but not reducible to it. Intergenerational continuity and occupational endogamy, for instance, seemed to occur. Indeed, typical participants of these circuits presented themselves or discussed their own trajectories in terms of a distinct social identity, the bicho-de-obra identity. The understanding of this social category and its related social identity became crucial for the analysis of large-scale projects as a form of production that generate their own internal dynamics.

*Becoming a bicho-de-obra.* Like many migrants, a person entering the large-scale project migratory circuit is mainly driven by the possibility of having access to better economic opportunities and, ideally, of saving money to enhance the quality of life of his or her domestic group. The would-be bicho-de-obra conceives of what is actually the first step of a long migratory sequence as a temporary move. Most often, the hardships of the surrounding environments at large-scale project sites together with the peculiarities of living in isolated company-towns are factors deterring individuals from conceiving of their coming experience as permanent as far as their work lives are concerned.

Whether a certain migratory experience is permanent or temporary is an important issue that has been analyzed in different migratory contexts. It has been shown, for instance, that a substantial part of Portuguese migrant labor also conceives of its stay in Germany as a temporary one, despite the fact that "going back home" is either a decision constantly postponed or that is never made (Klimt 1987a, 1987b). Concerning large-scale projects, though, it must be said once more that *temporariness* is a central dimension of these undertakings—works are actually finished, forcing segments of the labor force to move from one site to another.

Italian temporary migrant labor can be considered as having a "target earner" perspective, an expression Michael Piore (1979) uses to qualify migrants motivated to accomplish pragmatic economic goals in order to achieve upward social mobility in their home countries. Janet Schreiber, in her book on Italian temporary worker migration, states that laborers "defined the situation in the host country as a passing state of relative unimportance compared with the benefits it would provide them when they returned to their home community. A migrant who is focused upon resolving his status position and demonstrating his personal adequacy for his significant others does not plan his goals in terms of the area to which he migrates. He is migrating to maximize his conditions and family status in the place of origin, not the place of immigration, and his actions are consequent to this interpretation'' (Schreiber 1975, 268).

But, these migrants' experiences also create difficulties for their readjustment in the local village setting. In a section called the ''Emigration Mentality,'' William Douglas (1984, 107–8), describing the Italian returnee's ''difficult, and frequently unsuccessful, readjustment'' quotes the following passage by Masciotta: ''The few years spent in America as a laborer make him a demanding man, a man who has need of beer, of liqueurs, of steak, and in the evening even of a little bit of theater or horse racing. Returned amongst us with many new needs, few of which he can satisfy here, he feels nostalgia for foggy Pennsylvania or Canada, and he no longer works with desire because he finds the work to be almost uncompensated. And thus, having spent the savings scraped together abroad in the town taverns, he once again procures a passport for a second or third voyage'' (Giambattista Masciotta 1914, *Il Molise dalle Origini ai Nostri Giorni,* vol. 1, Naples, 345).

It is hard, and perhaps impossible, to demarcate from the outset the limits of a migrant's definition of the economic rewards for which he is searching. Goals often expand once the migrant enters the circuit. It is not uncommon to find amongst the skilled segment of Yacyretá's labor force bichos-de-obra who have fulfilled their previous economic goals, usually by making investments in their home countries and accumulating a sizable quantity of money, but who nonetheless do not want to leave the circuit. On one hand, this means that the logic of the occupation has taken over the initial intentions behind the trajectory of these migrants. In fact, the idea of a career in engineering, for instance, may naturalize a person's understanding of the occupational migratory circuit. On the other hand, there are other factors that intervene. I will first consider how the logic of the occupation may restrain a person from leaving the large-scale project migratory circuit. I will then describe mechanisms that refer to broader social determinants.

First, a person that has participated in a large-scale project acquired an occupational background that made him a specialist in certain tasks or a desirable commodity in the large-scale projects' market. It is very likely, thus, that this person either will consider participating in another project or will be convinced by his employers, in case he considers leaving the circuit, with the offer of a better wage or a better position in the next job. Furthermore, since large-scale projects are the cream of the construction industry market, their wages and fringe benefits are already highly attractive. When a person leaves a large-scale project on-site job and considers getting back to an urban occupation, it is hard to find equally rewarding jobs in his home town or country. It is likely that he will find that the wages available cannot match those he was used to receiving, especially if fringe benefits such as free housing are considered. Moreover, since this person has been for several years working in an isolated area, he has lost access to the social networks that would facilitate his entrance in a given urban labor market. In these crucial moments of a person's labor trajectory, it is common to decide to become engaged in another large-scale project. Projects are temporary jobs at any rate.

At this point, a major restructuring of the subjectivity and intersubjectivity of the would-be bicho-de-obra is already under way. The main reason is the loss of the social networks that this person used to have "back home." He begins to become a nonmeaningful concrete actor to his previous social networks, an image, a memory. This gradual process unfolds through various times and decisions by the migrant. Going "back home" to reaffirm his membership to his original social network is usually what the young bicho-de-obra does during vacation time. Gradually he begins to perceive two related things: (1) his vacations are becoming mandatory visits to the houses of relatives with different psychological and social costs for himself and his family; (2) he is losing his meaning as a social actor in the broader social network he identifies as his original one. The passage of time tends to intensify the unfolding of this process. The already bicho-de-obra increasingly realizes that the quality of his membership in the original network is changing and is problematic. He begins to conceive of himself as "uprooted." Visiting his family and home town becomes a secondary option during his vacations. He wants to have *real* vacations, he wants to rest from his work.

Parallel to this process of loss of a migrant's previous social identity, there develops a new process of identification. The large-scale project camp slowly becomes "home." He begins to consider the people he interacts with on a daily basis in the project environment as his main social network. Ambiguity installs itself. The bicho-de-obra is still an individual from a certain country, or from a certain province, but he feels like a stranger when he goes back to his original place. Some friends and relatives have died; others have changed their positions within the kinship system (marriages, divorces, births). An unmarried migrant might have gotten married to a woman of the country where the construction is being carried out. In their "homelands," these migrants face the results of the unfolding of developmental cycles of many domestic groups. Since they could not follow those unfoldings as active members of these social networks, they find that their original place is not the same anymore.

Indeed, getting out of a given social network for a lengthy period of time means the impossibility of accompanying the daily, multiple, and different interactions that make social actors meaningful to each other because of their sharing of the intricate webs of intersubjective interactions on a regular basis. What is difficult to estimate here is the amount of time this process takes to unfold fully. It certainly varies according to individuals. During my research in Yacyretá, I was frequently led to consider whether the reasons for becoming a bicho-de-obra (beyond professional-economic considerations) were not also related to conflictive relationships being developed by the would-be migrant within his original network. Furthermore, being originally from small cities or disliking large urban environments was another recurrent characteristic among some of these people.

In reality, the migrant's *practical consciousness* is undergoing radical changes. Practical consciousness is a notion elaborated by Anthony Giddens (1984) to refer to the routinization of social actions and the predictability that it entails in daily social interactions. It is a basic constituent of social actors because it allows for a necessary margin of predictability in individuals' mutual monitoring of their actions, and it conveys a sense of security and stability to the system of interactions. Giddens considers that "routinization is vital to the psychological mechanisms whereby a sense of trust or ontological security is sustained in the daily activities of social life. Carried primarily in practical consciousness, routine drives a wedge between the potentially explosive content of the unconscious and the reflexive monitoring of action which agents display" (Giddens 1984, xxiii). Practical consciousness is a characteristic of the social life of people everywhere. In this sense, it may be true that an expatriate loses, for instance, the practical consciousness of the small Italian town, but he "acquires" another: that of the large-scale project migratory circuit.

*"Neither meat nor fish": being a bicho-de-obra.* Some of the labels these migrants use to classify themselves, such as *uprooted, expatriate,* and *gypsies,* are indicative of their being conscious of the migratory experience working in a large-scale project implies. Furthermore, they also indicate a perception that combines nomadism and ambiguity. *Uprooted,* for instance, is the most frequent category that Argentine participants of the large-scale project migratory circuit use to classify their experience. Its metaphorical power alludes to the loss of a previous stable, grounded situation that is replaced by a new environment where readaptation is mandatory if one is to survive it. Since the Argentines are working in their own country, nationality is not the apparent issue it is for expatriates. *Expatriate* also alludes to a loss, in this case of a fatherland, and tends to approximate negative connotations such as forced resettlement or exile. In this sense, both *uprooted* and *expatriate* allude to experiences that social actors wish would be temporary. Nevertheless, *gypsy,* a category frequently used by participants of both the national and international migratory circuits, is indicative of the assumption of temporariness as permanent, of being a member of a nomadic life-style. Indeed, this is the case for many bichos-de-obra.

In Yacyretá, I met several individuals who had spent their whole career within the large-scale project migratory circuit. I was told about the existence of people like these who were living in other work sites. In Yacyretá, their trajectories varied according to whether they were in the Argentine or international circuits. But most of them had had six or more participations in large-scale projects, in a manner similar to a long step-migration chain. Furthermore, many had raised their children in different large-scale projects in Argentina or around the world. I met third-generation bichos-de-obra, a clear demonstration of intergenerational continuity.

For a family living in a large-scale project, the crucial time is when its young members have to leave the circuit for educational or occupational reasons. In Yacyretá, for instance, and amongst the Italian segment, this may happen twice. The first time is when the child is entering secondary-level training. Despite the existence of Italian schools in all projects in which they have participated, some people thought that their children could have a better education "back home." The separation of parents and teenagers is common. Indeed, there are few teenagers in Yacyretá's Villa Permanente or Mil Viviendas. If the teenager has remained with his or her parents and attends the camp's school, the hard separation decision for these migrant families may be faced later when the teenager finishes his or her secondary training. At this point, the teenager will either have to follow higher education or go to work. Going "back home" is a solution, too. Nevertheless, the presence of second and even third-generation bichos-de-obra in Yacyretá shows that not all of them leave the system. Furthermore, and more interestingly, it is not uncommon to leave it and come back.

Indeed, in one family whose members had been exposed to large-scale projects for more than three decades, all the children were working or living in different projects around the world. One of them had married another participant in the project migratory circuits, an occurrence that is not uncommon. It is interesting to note that although they are second-generation participants in this migratory process, like other migrants that conceive of their experiences as temporary (Klimt 1987a), they think of Italy as their "homeland." In this case, the role that mutual-aid associations play in the maintenance of migrant identities (see Maeyama 1979; Szuchman 1980) is performed by services the corporation provides such as the distribution of Italian papers and videotapes and, more importantly, by the camp school. The European segment of the labor force also celebrates national holidays in their Club Hípico. Interestingly enough, Uruguayans, a sizable foreign population in Yacyretá, did not count on a separate school for their children, but they did rely on their mutual-aid association.

I met young people who had tried to live in Italy, out of the project's environment, but had failed. They said they knew they were not like the other Italians; they were not satisfied with the provincial vision of the world Italian youth seemed to have, or with the low wages and extremely competitive daily lives to which they had to adjust. They also considered that after living for so long under a corporation's influence, they had become "corporation brats." They had been spoiled by Servicios Generales, the community action department of the contractor, and they had been given more attention than children in other contexts because of their parents feeling guilty for raising them in adverse circumstances. In fact, if something breaks in a project camp, for instance, one calls General Services to fix it immediately, free of charge. General Services also takes care of your documents and travel tickets, something important for a population that is constantly traveling. For the skilled segment of the labor force the sense of "Big Brother is watching you," mentioned by Murphy (1983, 167), goes along with a sense of "Big Brother is helping you," or, better, of "company paternalism," something typical of industries that immobilize a labor force via housing (Tilly 1985, Leite Lopes 1979).

After several years of feeling like strangers in Italy, the young adults I spoke with decided that they belonged on construction sites, and reentered the circuit. A young woman who had spent her whole life at large-scale projects and was about to return to Italy, doubted whether she would remain in Europe. She considered making an attempt because she could always go back to a project to work in the corporation's on-site office. A young Argentine man, a second-generation large-scale project migrant and the father of two children, also deemed he would hardly leave the circuit. These examples are not exclusive to the second generation of bichos-de-obra. Cases of first-generation individuals who had failed to settle down in an urban environment at some point of their migratory sequences were frequently reported. The explanations for these failures varied from the inability to readapt to urban environments (although large-scale project housing areas resemble small villages, they represent unique residential experiences), to the absence of a daily life marked both by a clear-cut structure of privileges and the synergy of large-scale construction projects.

Indeed, life and work at construction sites also involve a great deal of outdoor activity, hectic interaction, cooperation with several labor teams, and a clear sense of accomplishment. Most of the professionals, technicians, and workers described their jobs as fulfilling a need for concrete achievement. As an engineer told me: "when we come to a place there is nothing. While we are working we see the transformation and accumulation of our work. Once we are finished, it is as if we face dead work. It is time to move again." The professionals talked about nature as a powerful entity that needed to be understood in order to be tamed. Damming a river is seen as a challenge taken to benefit the progress of civilization. Engineers, technicians, and foremen are also powerful actors at projects' sites, sometimes commanding hundreds of men. Barabas (1977) describes the transformation of engineers into the Messiah, an image conjured up by a messianic movement of natives affected by a hydroelectric project in Mexico.

Intergenerational continuity and the potential for bicho-de-obra inbreeding, or occupational endogamy, are factors that reinforce a conceptualization of those workers as a permanent migratory population, attracted and created by the logic of large-scale projects' migratory circuits in national or international scales. In this sense, it does not matter whether retiring individuals leave the circuits. They will carry their identities in ways analogous to retired military personnel or diplomats. As long as large-scale projects exist, bichos-de-obra will exist.

## Final Comments on Labor Market Segmentation: The Different Rotational Speeds of the Segments

A discussion of labor market formation that contemplates corporations' labor needs as well as migratory processes and their associated social changes, prompts a complex and dynamic vision of the labor market, one where several processes unfold with distinct rhythms and directions among the various segments occupying different positions. I hope the analysis of Yacyretá's labor market showed that the project merges local, regional, national, and international populations, albeit in different positions and with different consequences. For the sake of this study, it was important to conceptualize the labor market as analytically divided into skilled and unskilled segments of the labor force and, simultaneously, crossed by ethnic segmentation. It was such a conceptualization that led to an interpretation of the several segments of Yacyretá's labor market as linked to different processes of labor flow and social change, segments that were ultimately unified, although temporarily, by the galvanizing presence of the large-scale project.

The labor market can thus be understood as being structured by processes of proletarianization affecting the local population; by processes of labor recruitment affecting local, regional, and, potentially, national populations that participate in organized labor flows and enter migratory labor systems; and by processes whereby an internal market is created in which national and international populations enter large-scale projects' migratory circuits and become bichos-de-obra. Evidently, given the possibilities for upward mobility for an individual, there is a flow between these different layers of the labor market. For instance, a person that became proletarianized through employment in a particular large-scale project may become a skilled worker and, potentially, a bicho-de-obra.

*Internal markets* is a notion that Portes and Bach use to analyze oligopolistic corporations. It is partially appropriate to understand the characteristics of a structured labor market permanently attached to large-scale projects:

> *Internal markets* means the division of work into finely graded job ladders. Hiring is generally at the bottom, and access to higher positions is usually through internal promotion rather than external recruitment. Stability is promoted by the fact that workers confront not the arbitrary orders of a boss or foreman, but rather a set of explicitly laid-out rules. More importantly, job ladders offer the incentive to remain with a particular firm, since seniority and training are rewarded with increases in pay and status. Oligopolistic corporations are able to create internal markets because of their size and because they can compensate for increases in labor costs with increases in productivity, higher prices for the final product, or both. Wages in this sector of the economy are thus higher and fringe benefits and work conditions more desirable.'' (Portes and Bach 1985, 17)

Spatial mobility is an important feature of large-scale projects related to their temporariness that, in turn, is a result of the multiple displacements of capital and labor required by the production process in the large-scale engineering industry. The crossing of spatial mobility with the different type of structure of the labor market made it possible to see not only that migratory processes and associated social changes are not the same for all segments of the labor market, but a segment's permanence in a specific large-scale project or within the migratory labor flows they cause is also differentiated. If large-scale projects are considered dyachronically we would see that the higher one goes in the labor market structure the longer a segment will stay connected with the large-scale project migratory circuit; the lower segment tends, on the contrary, to have unique experiences with large-scale projects. If a project is considered alone, as one event that is not part of a synchronic or dyachronic chain, the higher one goes in the labor market structure the shorter the time-span in which a segment will remain within a specific large-scale project. The lower one goes, the longer a segment will stay in the same project, and the more likely it will be demobilized, returning to its previous occupations or entering migratory labor flows other than the large-scale project migratory circuit. This is what I call the differential speed of rotations of the labor market segments. It ranges from a situation where spatial mobility, over the years, is almost none, to a situation wherein every two to five years a move occurs.

In reality, there are groups constantly attached to large-scale projects that experience even shorter periods within a given project. The so-called task forces, for instance, are groups of highly specialized technicians that have short assignments in a project, most of the time to solve specific questions or to mount and install sophisticated equipment. Their permanence in a project can vary from periods of a few weeks to a few months. Primo Levi (1987), in his novel *The Monkey's Wrench,* gives a literary account of a typical Italian bicho-de-obra who participated in several task forces.

Undoubtedly, *experts* form the group developing the highest speed within this system. They are a small minority of professionals based in world centers, highly specialized in sophisticated problem solving (river closure, for instance) who stay at a project for a few days or weeks. Their activity would typically involve brain storming with the technical elite of the project, site inspection, and the preparation of reports. Experts rely on the comparative knowledge they have been able to develop at various large-scale projects. In this sense, the more projects an expert has visited, the more expert he or she will be.

Besides the fact that the activities mentioned involve different kinds of labor, there can be a relationship between rotational speed and economic rewards. In fact, if we reduce our argument to the professional group of the skilled segment, it seems to be that, over a sequence of projects, the least amount of time a person stays in a project the higher the rewards.

The analysis of the Yacyretá project has showed that its internal differentiation relates to a hierarchy of positions determined by the project's division of labor *and* by the concrete contexts where project labor needs are defined. The latter are not a priori defined by a pure consideration of the technical needs of the production process. As we know, Yacyretá's labor needs were conditioned by legal instruments, such as the Yacyretá Treaty and its labor protocol; by political processes underlying the awarding of the YC-1 contract and the creation of ERIDAY, the main contractor; by the fact that the lead firms of the main contractor are Italian and French; and by its location in a relatively populated area, something that allowed the recruitment of local people as unskilled labor.

# 6 Conclusion

## Transnational Integration and the Controversy on Development

The study of the Yacyretá Dam provided a powerful opportunity to investigate several issues connected to the expansion of economic systems in the contemporary world: the articulation of international, national, regional, and local elites; the importance of subcontracting, "consortiation," as the political and economic process through which articulation and expansion occur; the complex relationships between national political-economy and transnational interests operating within the world-system; developmental cycles associated with huge supralocal economic initiatives and the dynamics they cause; occupational migratory flows, on national and global scales; the socioeconomic impact of a large-scale project on local reality; the creation of a new social identity intimately related to the logics of transnational capitalism.

But, here, rather than summarizing previous arguments, I will conclude by addressing two of most important issues underlying this book, which are expressed by two questions that I tried to examine in consistent terms with the help of first-hand ethnographic data. How will the growing integration of the contemporary world be interpreted? Do development projects promote development? Although these are simple questions to pose, they surely have no simple answer.

## The Shrinking of the World and Fragmentation of Identities

It is almost a truism to consider that the world is integrating at an increasingly accelerated pace. In anthropology, this discussion, explicitly or not, has been approached within a framework that articulates a vision of the "shrinking" of the world with one of a growing participation of populations within the world-system. It is now clear that the tension between heterogeneous and homogeneous human realities need to be analyzed in a field of contradictions created by globalist and localist forces.

The powerful changes the world is undergoing in this era of "flexible accumulation" (Harvey 1989), a different moment in capitalist history, have prompted several new political, economic, and sociocultural phenomena. Relationships between local and supralocal processes, a traditional focus of anthropological research, are now subject to different historical and sociological contexts. To contribute to the understanding of different political and economic aspects of the local-supralocal relationships, as the world system is at the present time, I constructed the notion of "consortiation." But there are equally important emergent sociocultural realities that should be interpreted such as the growth of ambiguity in culture, the ephemerality of social relations, transnationalism, "deterritorialization," that is, the clear loss of sui generis relationships between territory and culture, and the fragmentation of identities. Under the present conditions, fragmentation, for instance, is taken to paroxysm because it is often impossible to map the origin of the cultural referents with which many actors of mass societies live. Since I consider that anthropology's strongest contributions to social theory were most often based on ethnographic examples, my arguments here are directly inspired by the experience of the bichos-de-obra, or "work-site animals," described in last chapter.

George Marcus correctly considers that identity formation is one of the main issues that needs to be understood to comprehend the present time (Marcus 1990, 4). For Marcus, "identity processes in modernity concern a 'homeless mind' that cannot be permanently resolved as coherent or as a stable formation in theory or in social life itself" (Marcus 1990, 7). Indeed, time and space, notions that are fundamental in the formation of social actors' subjectivities and, consequently, in the formation and differentiation of identities and cultures, for several decades have been going through radical transformations that unfold faster and faster and whose effects are typically felt by the inhabitants of mass societies (Harvey 1989). Other implications of the present state of integration of the world-system are the increasing ethnic diversity under the umbrella of a similar set of powerful constraints and the acceleration of the circulation of people, things, and information on a global scale. *Ethnic segmentation* of the labor market and *time-space compression* are two notions useful to interpret these processes.

The notion of "ethnic segmentation of the labor market" was already explored in the book *Europe and the People without History* (Wolf 1982, 379–81). It is a systemic notion that takes into account global migratory processes provoked by the expansion of capitalism and shows how different ethnic groups occupy positions that may vary in historical time. This concept condenses historical and anthropological visions of the structured formation of contemporary human populations and shows that with capitalist development the complexity of the arrangements of ethnic segmentation increased enormously, creating interethnic systems with multiple alterities. The proximity and interdependence of differences are factors that contribute both to the perception of the shrinking of the contemporary world and to the fragmentation of individual perceptions, in a double movement of homogenization and heterogenization that occurs as a consequence of the simultaneous exposure to a "same" shared reality, by clearly different perspectives.

My analysis of Yacyretá dealt with the growing integration of the world considering the ethnic segmentation of the project's labor market and the articulation of different levels of integration. But, both processes occur in a context structured by the present conditions of *time-space compression,* an all-encompassing notion developed by David Harvey (1989) that is highly instrumental to understanding the "shrinking of the world" caused by capitalist expansion, especially by the development of systems of transportation, communication, and information. These developments contributed to an increase in the fragmented perception of the world by offering the inhabitant of mass societies a quantity of stimuli and information on a scale without precedent. Harvey also considers (a) the great speed of circulation both of fixed and variable capitals on a planetary scale, something that contributes substantially to increase the atmosphere of "volatility," and (b) changes in managerial ideologies with the passage from Fordism to flexible accumulation, a type of accumulation that benefits from the advantages of the annihilation of global space through time.

Time-space compression is a process with unequal intensity and development in its social and spatial distributions. It is also an experience of perception, a symbolic experience. In fact, the size of the world is the same. For most of the people, it is only presented and perceived as smaller, especially given the action of the mass media. Those who experience and live the shrinking, that is, who are social actors that directly foster or suffer it, are a relative minority. The world appears *as if* it had shrunk while it is evidently of the same size. The novelty is that it can be experienced as if it really had diminished. Its several fragments are presented in a condensed way, frequently articulated as in a patchwork while bombarding individuals with information and stimuli on an unprecedented scale.

Work-site animals richly illustrate different angles of the problem under discussion. They are people who leave a context in which, although their identities were fragmented in a modern sense, they had not yet entered a circuit of acceleration of the fragmentation and annihilation of the space through the conditions of time-space compression typical of "flexible accumulation." Furthermore, work-site animals often comprise a transnational population working for transnational corporations, another powerful actor in the present scenario.

### Deterritorialization, Identity Fragmentation, and Ambiguity

To further develop my arguments I shall return to some of the characteristics of work-site animals already exposed. Work-site animals are "deterritorialized" people in the sense that they lose the possibility of realizing a univocal identification between territory, culture, nation, and identity, a fact expressed in the labels they use to describe themselves: uprooted, expatriated, gypsies, citizens of the world. Nevertheless, since daily human activities need a place or a set of places definable as a "territory" in which, with a greater or lesser degree of stability, fundamental actions for reproducing a life-style can unfold, work-site animals live as if the territories of large-scale projects, their camps, and the small villages of the world system were theirs, a space made homogeneous by the process of capitalist expansion. Their cultural deterritorialization is fulfilled by a territorialization defined by the labor sphere, a fact expressed in the label *work-site animal.*

The residential area of a large-scale project is a space, without a culturally sui generis identity, that intends to reproduce the totality of an urban environment. It is planned and managed by a central bureaucracy and organized by constraints clearly defined by the interests of agencies linked to the necessities of flexible accumulation. Therefore, the qualities of the spatial organization of different projects are the "same," delimited by the necessities of the production processes in a way that its structure is repeated in any part of the world. In this sense, it is *as if* it were the same for the work to be in Argentina, Pakistan, or Nigeria.

In such a universe, the transnational corporation tries to maximize flexible accumulation and fosters time-space compression with the accelerated turnover of its employees within the circuits of the world system. The corporation ends up being the principal organizer of the formal processes of socialization, such as the creation and maintenance of the set of factors determining the Italian facets of the work-site animal identity. In this way, in a world where the contradictions between globalism and localism are many and have affected the system of nation-states in several ways (see Szentes 1988), in the context of a large-scale project the transnational corporation becomes responsible for the maintenance of mechanisms of reproduction and fixing of national identities in a situation of strong ethnic segmentation. It is the corporation that circulates information from Italy (videos, magazines, and newspapers) and promotes or stimulates the celebration of national and religious holidays. More importantly, it is the corporation that manages the Italian school, a fundamental place for the socialization of the children of the work-site animals, where phenomena of the "as if" type develop increasing cultural ambiguity. A child studies to be an Italian citizen *as if* he or she were in Italy, provoking visible mismatches between the transmission of a national identity that should be processed within the school and the reality experienced in the project's territory.

Other equally important examples are related to the characteristics created by the ethnic segmentation and by the large-scale project migratory circuits that get reflected in the structuring of the domestic group such as interethnic families, bilingualism, and multilingualism. In this context, not only linguistic ambivalence arises, but also a higher exposure to cultural fragmentation. In the end, Italy represents a formative past identity almost only for the father of the family. For mother and children it is a foreign country, a special one without any doubt, but a country that is not directly experienced and is most often conceived through institutions, such as the school and the corporation, or through political kin and other work-site animals of Italian origin.

In the case of children of Italian couples, although exposed for years to Italian schools in the camps, ambiguity was also present since they did not identify themselves with what they supposed to be typical Italian young-sters. Their daily social networks are marked by the total experience of living in large-scale project environments.

The analysis of the experience of the work-site animals led to several conclusions. The processes of socialization internal to the domestic group, to a great extent responsible for the construction of individual identities, are affected by the situation of immobilization of the labor force through housing and by other overall characteristics of large-scale projects, espe-cially those that were highlighted and related to ethnic segmentation and to the participation in large-scale projects' international migratory circuits. The work-site animal ends up assuming as a fundamental dimension of his or her identity the facets associated with the labor sphere. Although the basic agencies of identity formation are present, they were hegemonized by the world of labor given the conditions of time-space compression experi-enced by this population.

Nevertheless, it is evident that a work-site animal of Italian origin is different from one of French origin. For this reason, I propose that the agencies and processes responsible for identity formation (the ones related to family and school life, for instance) keep their efficacy. But work-site animals are in a situation where there is a change in the relative powers of structuration of the agencies and processes involved in identity formation. These people live in a situation hegemonized by the characteristics of the work universe where their daily lives unfold. In this context of high fragmentation and of deterritorialization, we find a social actor dominated by a professional occupation, tending to be disembodied from a cultural and ethnic identity, and conceiving of her- or himself as a citizen of the world, a citizen of a world-system increasingly more homogeneous despite the fact that or perhaps because of it—it promotes the interaction and integration of heterogeneous population segments.

*Identity fragmentation* needs, therefore, to be understood in a universe where there is a growing acceleration of changes of the contexts of social and communicative encounters and a multiple exposure to socializing and normative agencies, that are also traveling in an accelerated flow of changes. In this situation, identities can only be defined as being a synthesis of multiple alterities constructed from a great number of interactive contexts regulated, most of the time, by institutions. That is, instead of an irreducible essence, identity, under certain conditions of time-space compression and within some regions of complex societies, can be conceived as a multifaceted flow subject to negotiations and rigidity, to greater or lesser degree, according to the interactive contexts that most of the time are institutionally regulated by a socializing or normative agency (for a similar position, see Marcus 1990, 29).

On one hand, fragmentation is a reality that structures the subject. On the other hand, it is a set that is characteristic of the subject, but that undergoes constant change in a way that one of its multiple facets, or an aggregate of them, may be hegemonic in relationship to the others according to the contexts. Under conditions of extreme change, the defining arrangement of collective and individual identities may go through radical transformations, even leading to a redefinition, to a *reconstruction* of the general characteristics of the (open) totality and of the relationships of hegemony between its constitutive parts (facets).

Finally, the situations of copresence with representatives of other identities, especially ethnic identities, are essential to suggest or to define, via the classic mechanism of contrast made explicit by difference, a possible repertoire of alliances in situations of cooperation or conflict. In this sense, the processes that arise in interethnic systems are political, cultural, linguistic, and also pertain to the domain of kinship such as interethnic marriages, exchange of women. In turn, these processes are fundamental to the reinforcement or to the reconstruction of identitites. Greater ethnic segmentation corresponds with greater fragmentation provoked by the the interethnic system and with the greater importance of processes associated with this situation in social actors' daily lives.

## Do Development Projects Promote Development?

In the present book, I was guided by the conviction that although the complexity of the issues involved often transcended the frontiers of anthropological work, I should neither restrain myself from addressing them nor avoid the possible contributions—controversial, perhaps—that this work could have for a discussion of development. During field research I often came face to face not only with the impersonal aspects of capitalist accumulation, but also with a clash of conceptions on what development is or should be. Large-scale projects such as Yacyretá will always generate a multiplicity of viewpoints on the part of planners and participants. It is thus one of the tasks of the anthropologist to do justice to the numerous, often conflicting visions.

The process undergirding the decision to construct a hydroelectric project such as Yacyretá is highly marked by claims to legitimacy firmly grounded in developmentalist ideas that conceive of economic growth as a steady unilinear movement to be initiated or enhanced by the presence of a large-scale project. The legitimation effort can be described as a set of discourses frequently obscured by technicalities. They may vary from sophisticated analyses where a project naturally appears as the least-expensive solution for a long-awaited necessity to the sheer belief that the mere availability of a factor of production, in this case energy, will promote development by itself. Since projects are often carried out in isolated areas, another common way of legitimating them is to state that they also promote regional development.

However strongly the promoters of "development projects" emphasize their economic rationality and need, their tendency to underplay class differences and the political factors intervening in development planning fosters a vision that is clearly biased. I consider the legitimation effort—carried out before, during, and after the execution of a project—to be a key characteristic of large-scale projects, because it is directly responsible for generating the ideology that *that project* is the best and most reasonable solution for an economic or social problem of national or regional scope. The acceptance and promotion of a project is embedded in an ideological universe ruled by notions such as progress and development.

## Considerations on Progress and Development

*Development* is one of the most inclusive notions in a general sense and within the specialized literature. Its importance for the organization of social, political, and economic relations led anthropologists to consider it not only as "one of the basic ideas in modern West European culture" (Dahl and Hjort 1984, 166), but also "something of a secular religion," unquestioned, since "to oppose it is a heresy almost always severely punished" (Maybury-Lewis 1990, 1). The amplitude of this notion ranges from individual rights of citizenship to schemes of classification of nation-states within the world-system. It may encompass the attribution of value to change, tradition, social justice, welfare, mankind's destiny; the accumulation of economic, political, and military power; and many other connotations linked to ideals of proper men-men or men-nature relations.

The scope and multiple facets of development are what allow its many appropriations and sometimes divergent readings. The variation of the appropriations of the idea of development as well as the attempts to reform it are expressed in the numerous adjectives that are part of its history: industrial development, capitalist, socialist, inward, outward, community, unequal, dependent, and, currently, sustainable. These variations and tensions are indicative of the dynamics of a political and economic power field where collective actors strive to establish their particular perspectives on development as the most correct ones.

In fact, development is a plastic category that not only changes according to history, but also may be borne by different and opposite social segments. Attempts to reform this central ideology and utopia of the modern world practically begin with its arrival in the nineteenth century at the forefront of the scene as a consequence of political, social, economic, and philosophical unfoldings of the eighteenth century.

Development has many connotations associated with its main matrix, the idea of progress, a conception that according to historians and philosophers dates back to Ancient Greece (Delvaille 1969, Dodds 1973). The idea of progress becomes central and dominant as part of the new social contract and ideological universe accompanying the industrial revolution and the rise to power of the bourgeoisie in the eighteenth century with the consequent and impressive development of the production forces, especially the development of technology. As part of the processes of secularization and rationalization that unfolded in the nineteenth century, development—the twin idea of progress—and the possibility of rationally intervening in social processes became an explicit ideology of ruling elites, including intellectuals. For discussions related to these issues, see Dodds (1973), Hildebrand (1949), Delvaille (1969), and Binder (1986).

It is interesting to note, without entering a complex discussion on the status of "progress" as a civilizational matrix, that the idea of progress is based, on one level, on the perception—and on the subsequent analogical extension of this perception—that living beings experience growth in order to mature. In this connection, the idea of progress comes together, explicitly or not, with its opposite and complementary idea, that of decadence. It is as if humanity were permanently facing a dilemma between growing or perishing. It is necessary to highlight here the belief that the future will always be better than the present and the past because of a series of meliorations and innovations that people will invent. If present time constitutes some kind of a better stage than that of the past, it is a rather complex question that needs to be examined in a historical and systematic way, encompassing several dimensions of social life. Nevertheless, there is little doubt that, in a domain such as the technological one, a series of advancements have been occurring with the passage of time. Perhaps this is one of the main reasons why the belief in the redemption of mankind through technological improvement is the backbone of development as ideology and utopia.

The tension underlying the interpretative and political conflict typical of the field where development issues are discussed may be referred to as a double facet of the Enlightenment—a crucial moment for the unfolding of the new economic, political, and social pacts of modernity and its associated ideologies (progress, industrialism, secularism, rationalization, individualism, for instance). This double facet is expressed in the conflict between those defending a project linked to instrumental reason, the source of processes of economic growth and accumulation based on the exploitation of unequal social classes, and those defending a historical reason mainly concerned with social justice (Quijano 1988).

There are two interrelated and integrative aspects of the notion of development that need to be emphasized. Since the nineteenth century, the increased pace of the integration of the world-system started to require an ideology and utopia that made sense of the unequal positions within the system without resorting to open domination like in colonial situations. This ideology could provide an explanation wherein people placed in lower levels would be able to "understand" their positions and believe that there is a solution for their backward situation. It is not by accident that development terminology usually involves the use of metaphors that refer to space or order in a hierarchical way: developed/underdeveloped, advanced/backward, First World/Third World. This hierarchy is instrumental to the belief that there is a point that may be reached following some kind of recipe kept, secretly or not, by those nation-states that lead the "race" for a better future.

The second integrative aspect to be emphasized is the concept of development as a universally aspired notion that provides a neutral label to refer to the process of accumulation on a global scale. For Celso Furtado (1978, 78), "the idea of development as international performance" does not take into consideration local social structures because, besides being a transplantation of industrial civilization, it is "a simple expression of a pact between internal and external groups interested in accelerating accumulation." By using the term *development,* instead of accumulation or expansion, an undesirable connotation is avoided: the difference of power between the units of the system (within or between nation-states) in economic, political, and military terms. This characteristic has been the cause of a tautology, a sort of "blame the victim" reasoning, that can be exemplified by an archetypical statement like the following: they are underdeveloped because they do not believe in development.

The great power that development has as an organizational ideology and utopia becomes reflected in its centrality in those discourses that inform two opposing visions of society: the liberal capitalist discourse and the socialist one. Notwithstanding their evident differences, it is not incorrect to consider with Dahl and Hjort (1984, 176) that as "ideological constructs" both socialism and capitalism have an "economistic world view." For these authors, most socialist development policies imply "a strong commitment to the dominant meaning of the concept, based on growth, technological innovation, modernization and an assumed direct relation between these processes and human welfare." Furthermore, local autonomy or "the satisfaction of immaterial human needs," both in capitalism or socialism, are classified as "alternative models of development" (Dahl and Hjort, 1984).

Presently, given the changes in the political economy of the world-system and the consequent crisis of nineteenth-century rooted ideologies, environmentalism—a set of discourses with utopian and totalizing characteristics—has clearly become a recognized factor in the developmental drama. The importance of environmentalism is seen in its transformation into social movements and in its visible penetration in contemporary decision-making systems. Today it is an interlocutor accepted by the main participants (nation-states, multilateral agencies, managers, entrepreneurs, nongovernmental organizations, social movements) in the field of discussion on development (Ribeiro 1990).

With its increasing influence in the institutional milieu, environmentalists have had to compromise from a position that argued in terms of zero-growth toward a notion of sustainable development, which, in spite of the efforts under way, is still not completely elaborated or totally operational. This is the hard core around which powerful new attempts are increasingly trying to place environmentalism inside the economic, ideological, and political struggles for development (Ribeiro 1992). It represents, in a period of interpretive and political crisis, a different umbrella of alliances of environmentalists, governments, multilateral agencies, and corporate managers, where economic growth, the hard core of development, is not threatened (Ribeiro 1992).

In reality, there are many varieties of the environmentalist discourse. Like in other moments of the struggle for hegemony engendered by development these variations and tensions are representative of the logics of a field of political and economic power where collective actors strive to establish their particular perspectives as the correct ones.

For the magnitude of their technological, political, economic, social, and ecological characteristics, large-scale projects are major crossroads of developmental debate. In a large-scale project, development as ideology and utopia emerges in plenitude. Several discourses become entangled in complex ways under the hegemony of social actors, such as engineers, that have their worldview profoundly marked by their professional and technical trajectories as well as by the different alliances they make with representatives of industrial and financial capital. Other important variables in such a scenario are the developmental policies fostered by elites of the state and multilateral agencies often informed by different political and ideological positions. These positions may be present either in a diffused or organized fashion, through mass media or institutions such as unions and political parties.

Moreover, since each project creates its own power field, the main conflicts over what development is or should be are also clearly related to a project's particular political and economic dynamics.

## Development and the Moon Land

In Yacyretá, the discourses of "development promoters"—especially of those occupying powerful positions—often contrasted with those of local and regional leaders who claimed that the project was directed toward the Greater Buenos Aires area, that it had brought new social problems to the area, and, ultimately, the results of the project would just be a huge reservoir. This is a clear indication that the conceptions of progress and development are not homogeneous and even have different connotations for local and regional elites.

Indeed, the ways in which large-scale projects are structured internally—with various linkages among powerful public or private, national and transnational corporations—is a factor that limits the efficacy of most developmental claims on the part of their promoters. Two objective limitations stemming from the internal logic of large-scale projects were described in this book. First, the process of consortiation, a strategy of articulation of different levels of capital (transnational, national, regional, and local) tends to stimulate the concentration of capital despite the fact that some smaller firms may be co-opted in the process and eventually grow. Second, the large-scale project migratory circuit, which is a type of labor flow linked to structural characteristics of large-scale projects such as their temporary character, points to the cyclical character of projects as investments carried out on a worldwide scale. Small segments of the local and regional populations may eventually be drawn into better labor market positions through the large-scale project migratory circuit, but then, these segments will move to other places.

The internal developmental contradictions of large-scale projects can be summarized as follows: "development projects" immobilize huge amounts of resources by concentrating them in a point in space; they drain the best human and natural resources of an area, and move them to another; finally, once the work is finished, the bulk of the investment that flowed into an area during the construction period will dry up, thus increasing the probability that intensive activity will be followed by an economic depression. In the case of hydroelectric dams such as Yacyretá, rivers are dammed, huge reservoirs are created that displace human populations and affect ecosystems, for the most part to generate energy to individual and industrial consumers located outside of the region where the natural resource lies.

But, there remains the question about the developmental impact that may be produced by the facilities once they start operating. Most of the times these facilities are linked to the national economy and are not designed to address local- and regional-level needs. This tends to reinforce the pre-existing economic disparities. But sometimes, as in the case of Yacyretá, whether the investment is profitable is highly controversial. To put it another way, it is common knowledge among specialists in the Argentine energy sector that Yacyretá was not the best investment for the sector. The reason for the implementation of the project lies more within the realm of politics than economics. Many Argentine specialists whom I interviewed claimed that better alternate solutions would have been to build smaller dams, to build the Paraná Médio dam on the same Paraná River but within Argentine territory (avoiding the problems caused by binationality), or to take advantage of the availability of gas in Patagonia, in the south of the country.

My analysis of Yacyretá led me to conclude that this project does not so much produce ''development'' as it constitutes a form of production linked to economic expansion. In this sense it represents an outpost of an economic system that is pivotal to several central places worldwide and within the Argentine territory. Moreover, it is the kind of outpost that does not furnish consistent and stable economic opportunities for the local and regional population. If the definition of development minimally includes active participation of local and regional social actors, sustainability, and continuation of growth over time, a large-scale project can hardly be conceptualized as a ''development'' project. This is why, from the regional and local perspective, it is hard to consider a large-scale project as a promoter of development, even in the restricted economic sense of the expression.

What is also at stake is a confrontation between a conception of development that overstresses physical mobilization of natural and human resources in a purely pragmatic economic sense and a conception that gives priority to the need of fulfilling the social needs of populations that are located in specific cultural and historical scenarios. The pragmatic mobilization of human and natural resources ends up reinforcing existing disparities because it favors competitors that, from start, can move more resources. This is why such a conception is favored by social actors who typically reproduce their lives within the circuits of a national political-economy or within the world-system. Local and regional social actors are bounded by a sense of history and culture that orients their visions of their social reality towards more parochial objectives. This is one reason why the prospect of economic change is not necessarily welcome. Change for whom and in what direction?

# Appendix

## Composition of the ERIDAY Consortium

The thirty-two firms in ERIDAY are divided into an Impregilo group and a Dumez one. The first thirteen firms in the list that follows compose the Impregilo group, the other nineteen the Dumez associates.

1. Impresit-Girola-Lodigiani IMPREGILO S.p.A., Milan, Italy
2. Dott. Ing. Giuseppe Torno e Co. S.p.A., Milan, Italy
3. Recchi S.p.A. Costruzioni Generali, Turin, Italy
4. Italstrade S.p.A., Milan, Italy
5. Compañía Constructora de El Chocón Impregilo Sollazo S.A., Buenos Aires, Argentina
6. Sollazo Hnos. S.A. Empresa Constructora Ind. y Com., Buenos Aires, Argentina
7. Supercemento S.A.I.C., Buenos Aires, Argentina
8. Conevial S.A.C.I.C.I.F., Buenos Aires, Argentina
9. Sideco Americana S.A.C.I.I.F. (ex Impresit Sideco S.A.C.I.I.F.), Buenos Aires, Argentina
10. Polledo S.A.I.C.F., Buenos Aires, Argentina
11. Benito Roggio e Hijos S.A., Buenos Aires, Argentina
12. Consorcio de Empresas Constructoras Paraguayas S.R.L., Asunción, Paraguay
13. Empresa Alvaro Palenga S.A., Montevideo, Uruguay

14. Dumez S.A., Nanterre, France

15. Ed. Zublin Ag., Duisburg, West Germany

16. Dyckerhoff & Widmann Ag., Munich, West Germany

17. Cogefar Costruzioni Generali S.p.A., Milan, Italy

18. José Cartellone Construcciones Civiles S.A., Buenos Aires, Argentina

19. E.A.C.A. S.A. de Construcciones, Buenos Aires, Argentina

20. CODI S.A. y BABIC S.A., Buenos Aires, Argentina

21. Petersen, Thiele y Cruz S.A. de Construcciones y Mandatos, Buenos Aires, Argentina

22. Marengo S.A., Buenos Aires, Argentina

23. Bridas S.A.P.I.C. y Tecno Bridas S.A. I.C.I.F., Buenos Aires, Argentina

24. SACIFI S.I.F.I.S.A., Asunción, Paraguay

25. Promotec S.A., Asunción, Paraguay

26. Emparcon S.R.L., Asunción, Paraguay

27. Compañía Integral de Construcciones y Asociados, Asunción, Paraguay

28. Empresa Constructora Atilio Heisecke S.A., Asunción, Paraguay

29. Electromec S.A., Asunción, Paraguay

30. Coservi S.A., Asunción, Paraguay

31. Arquitecto José Puentes y Asociados, Asunción, Paraguay

32. Ing. Francisco Scorza, Asunción, Paraguay

## Bidders Selected in December 1978 for the YE-1 Contract Bidding

There were three consortia: ACWEST, formed by Allis-Chalmers Corporation and Westinghouse (USA); Yacyretá-Apipé, formed by Siemens AG (West Germany), Energomachexport (USSR), and G.I.E. (Italy); Japan Consortium (Mitsubishi, Hitachi, Toshiba, Fuji) and Voith (West Germany).

Nine individual firms were also preselected: Alsthom (France); Ingra (Yugoslavia); Creusot Loire (France); Asea (Sweden); Boving and Company (England); Voest-Alpine AG (Austria); Elin-Union (Austria); Escher Wyss (Switzerland); Skodaexport (Czechoslovakia).

The following five participants were selected under conditions: Duro Felguera S.A. and La Maquinita Terrestre y Marítima S.A.; A.E.G. Telefunken (West Germany); Dominion Engineering Company (Canada); General Electric Co. (USA); Brown Boveri (Switzerland) (see EBY 1978, 19).

## Contractors Associated with the Preparation of the Project's Infrastructure on the Argentine Side

Consorcio de Empresas Correntinas (Intemec S.A.I.C.-C.I.A.S.A.-Clebaner Ing. Civil S.A. and Jacobo Levitzky, Ing. Civil); Tecsa S.A.; Consorcio Econar Riva; Cibelli Construcciones S.A.-Gennaro y Fernandez S.A. de I. y C. (see EBY 1978, 21). The Añá-Cuá bridge contract was awarded to an Argentine-Paraguayan consortium called CAPPAC, formed by Techint S.A., Argentina, and the following Paraguayan firms: Perez y Yampey Construcciones S.A., Compañía de Construcciones Civiles S.R.L., Campo Grande S.A., Techint Eng. Co. and Coservi S.A. (see EBY 1979, 21).

# References

Aspelin, Paul. 1982. "Too Much Light: Hydroelectrics Development in Brazil. Hydroelectrics in Central and South America." Anthropology Resource Center, Bulletin 11, Boston.

Aspelin, Paul, and Sílvio dos Santos. 1981. *Indian Areas Threatened by Hydroelectric Projects in Brazil.* Copenhagen: IWGIA.

Azpiazu, Daniel, Eduardo M. Basualdo, and Miguel Khavisse. 1986. *El Nuevo Poder Económico en la Argentina de los Años 80.* Buenos Aires: Editorial Legasa.

Barabas, Alícia Mabel. 1977. "Chinantec Messianism: The Mediator of the Divine." In *Western Expansion and Indigenous Peoples,* edited by Elias Sevilla-Casas. Netherlands: Mouton Publishers.

Bartolomé, Leopoldo J. 1984. "Forced Resettlement and the Survival Systems of the Urban Poor." *Ethnology* 3: 177–92.

Becker, David G. 1983. *The New Bourgeoisie and the Limits of Dependency: Mining, Class, and Power in "Revolutionary" Peru.* Princeton: Princeton University Press.

———. 1984. "Recent Political Development in Peru: Dependency or Postdependency?" *Latin American Research Review* 19: 225–42.

Betiol, Laércio. 1983. *Itaipú. Modelo Avançado de Cooperação Internacional na Bacia do Prata.* Rio de Janeiro: Editora da Fundação Getúlio Vargas.

Binder, Leonard. 1986. "The Natural History of Development Theory." *Comparative Studies in Society and History* 28: 3–33.

Bloch, Maurice. 1977. "The Disconnection between Power and Rank as a Process. An Outline of the Development of Kingdoms in Central Madagascar." In *The Evolution of Social Systems,* edited by J. Friedman and M. Rowlands. London: DuckWorth.

———. 1985. *Marxism and Anthropology.* Oxford: Oxford University Press.

Bonacich, E. 1972. "A Theory of Ethnic Antagonism: The Split-Labor Market." *American Sociological Review* 5: 533–47.

Botana, Helvio I. 1982. *El Caldero de Yacyretá*. Buenos Aires: Pena Lillo Editor.

Burawoy, Michael. 1976. "The Functions and Reproduction of Migrant Labor: Comparative Material from Southern Africa and the United States." *American Journal of Sociology* 5: 1050–87.

Cardoso de Oliveira, Roberto. 1967. "Problemas e Hipóteses Relativos à Fricção Interétnica: Sugestoões para uma Metodologia." *Revista do Instituto de Ciências Sociais* vol. 4, no. 1. Rio de Janeiro.

———. 1976. *Identidade, Etnia e Estrutura Social*. São Paulo: Livraria Pioneira Editora.

Cernea, Michael M. 1988. "Involuntary Resettlement in Development Projects. Policy Guidelines in World Bank-Financed Projects." *World Bank Technical Paper*, no. 80. Washington.

———. 1989. "Anthropology, Policy and Involuntary Resettlement." *British Association for Social Anthropology in Policy and Practice, Newsletter*, no. 4.

Chase-Dunn, Christopher K. 1982. "A World-System Perspective on Dependency and Development in Latin America." *Latin American Research Review* 12:166–71.

CIDY, Consultores Internacionales de Yacyretá. 1984. Informe Mensual. Servicios Contractuales de CIDY, no. 71, June.

Colson, Elizabeth. 1971. *The Social Consequences of Resettlement. The Impact of the Kariba Resettlement upon the Gwembe Tonga*. London: Manchester University Press.

Conklin, Margaret, and Daphne Davidson. 1986. "The IMF and Economic and Social Human Rights: A Case Study of Argentina, 1958–1985." *Human Rights Quarterly. Comparative and International Journal of the Sciences, Humanities and Law* 8(2): 227–69.

Da Rosa, J. Eliseo. 1983. "Economics, Politics, and Hydroelectric Power: The Paraná River Basin." *Latin American Research Review* 18(3): 77–107.

Dahl, Gudrun, and Anders Hjort. 1984. "Development as Message and Meaning." *Ethnos* 49: 165–85.

Dalton, George. 1971. "Introduction." In *Economic Development and Social Change*, edited by G. Dalton. New York: American Museum Sourcebooks in Anthropology.

Delvaille, Jules. 1969. *Essai sur l'Histoire de l'Idée de Progrès, jusqu'à la fin du XVIII siècle*. 1st ed. 1910. Genève: Slatkine Reprints.

Dodds, E. R. 1973. *The Ancient Concept of Progress, and Other Essays on Greek literature and Belief*. Oxford: Oxford University Press.

Douglas, William A. 1984. *Emigration in a South Italian Town. An Anthropological History*. New Brunswick, New Jersey: Rutgers University Press.

Duqué, Ghislaine. 1980. "Casa Nova: Interventions du Pouvoir et Stratégies Paysannes. Un Municipe du Sertao Bahiano à l'heure de la Modernisation." Doctoral Dissertation. Paris: Ecole des Hautes Etudes en Sciences Sociales.

EBY (Entidad Binacional Yacyretá). 1978, 1979, 1980, 1981, 1983, 1984. *Memória y Balance.*

———. 1986. *Tratado de Yacyretá y Normas Complementárias.* Buenos Aires/Asunción.

Evans, Peter. 1985. "After Dependency: Recent Studies of Class, State, and Industrialization." *Latin American Research Review* 20: 149–60.

Furtado, Celso. 1978. "Da Ideologia do Progresso à do Desenvolvimento." In *Criatividade e Dependência na Civilização Industrial.* Rio de Janeiro: Paz e Terra.

———. *A Fantasia Organizada.* 1985. Rio de Janeiro: Paz e Terra.

Gaggiano, Carlos J. Vidal. 1980. "Estudio Relativo a los Aspectos Laborales de Capacitación y de Recursos Humanos, Vinculados con la Construcción de la Represa Hidroeléctrica de Yacyretá-Apipé sobre el Río Paraná." Organización Internacional del Trabajo. Buenos Aires: Oficina Internacional del Trabajo.

Giddens, Anthony. 1984. *The Constitution of Society. Outline of the Theory of Structuration.* Berkeley: University of California Press.

Godelier, Maurice. 1977. "De la Non Correspondance entre Formes et Contenus des Rapports Sociaux. Nouvelle Réflexion sur l'exemple des Incas." In *Horizons, Trajets Marxistes en Anthropologie.* Paris: François Maspero.

Goffman, Erving. 1962. *Asylums: Essays on the Social Situation of Mental Patients and Other Inmates.* Chicago: Aldine Publishing.

Gordon, David M. 1972. *Theories of Poverty and Underemployment: Orthodox, Radical, and Dual Labor Market Perspectives.* Lexington, MA: Lexington Books, D.C. Heath.

Gross, Daniel. 1985. "Amazonia and the Progress of Ethnology." *Latin American Research Review* XX: 200–22.

Hansen, Art, and Anthony Oliver-Smith, eds. 1982. *Involuntary Migration. The Problems and Responses of Dislocated People.* Boulder: Westview Press.

Harris, Marvin. 1964. *Pattern of Races in the Americas.* New York: Waler and Company.

Harvey, David. 1989. *The Condition of Post-Modernity.* Oxford: Basil Blackwell.

Harza News. 1980. "Yacyretá Project." *Harza News* (Winter): 2–9.

Hildebrand, George H. 1949. "The Idea of Progress: An Historical Analysis." In *The Idea of Progress. A Collection of Readings,* edited by Frederick J. Teggart. Berkeley: University of California Press.

Hoben, Allan. 1982. "Anthropologists and Development." *Annual Review of Anthropology* 11: 349–75.

———. 1984. "The Role of the Anthropologist in Development Work: An Overview." In *Training Manual in Development Anthropology,* edited by William Partridge. Special Publication of the American Anthropological Association and the Society of Applied Anthropology, no. 17.

IBASE (Instituto Brasileiro de Análises Sociais e Econômicas). 1983. *Carajás: O Brasil Hipoteca seu Futuro.* Rio de Janeiro: Achiamé.

Khaldun, Ibn. 1969. *The Muqaddimah. An Introduction to History.* Princeton: Princeton University Press.

Kitching, Gavin. 1982. *Development and Underdevelopment in Historical Perspective. Populism, Nationalism and Industrialization.* New York: Methuen.

Klimt, Andrea. 1987a. " 'Temporary' and 'Permanent' Lives: Portuguese Migrants in Germany.'' Paper presented at the Sixth International Conference of Europeanists. Washington, D.C.

————. 1987b. "Building a 'Home'—Portuguese Migrant Notions of Temporariness, Permanence, and Commitment." Paper presented at the 86th Annual Meeting of the American Anthropological Association. Chicago.

Laurelli, Elsa. 1987. "Los Grandes Proyectos: Estratégias de Desarrollo y Transformación del Território." In *Los Grandes Proyectos y el Espacio Regional. Presas Hidroeléctricas y el sistema decisional.* Cuadernos del CEUR 19. Buenos Aires.

Lawson, Michael L. 1982. *Dammed Indians. The Pick-Sloan Plan and the Missouri River Sioux, 1944–1980.* Norman: University of Oklahoma Press.

Leite Lopes, José Sérgio. 1979. "Fábrica e Vila Operária: Considerações sobre uma Forma de Subordinação Burguesa." In *Mudança Social no Nordeste. A Reprodução da Subordinação.* Rio de Janeiro: Paz e Terra.

Levi, Primo. 1987. *The Monkey's Wrench.* New York: Penguin Books.

Maceyra, Horácio. 1986. "Cámpora, Perón, Isabel." In *Presidencias y Golpes Militares del Siglo XX.* Buenos Aires: Centro Editor de América Latina, S.A.

Maeyama, T. 1979. "Ethnicity, Secret Societies and Associations: The Japanese in Brazil." *Comparative Studies in Society and History* 21: 589–610.

Marcus, George. 1990. "Past, Present, and Emergent Identities: Requirements for Ethnographies of Late Twentieth Century Modernity Worldwide." Lecture delivered at the 17th Meeting of the Brazilian Anthropological Association. Florianópolis. Mimeo.

Marcus, George, and Michael M. J. Fischer. 1986. *Anthropology as Cultural Critique. An Experimental Moment in the Human Sciences.* Chicago: University of Chicago Press.

Marx, Karl. 1977. *Capital: A Critique of Political Economy.* New York: Random Press.

Maybury-Lewis, David. 1990. "Development and Human Rights. The Responsibility of the Anthropologist." Paper presented at the International Seminar on Development and Human Rights. Brazilian Anthropological Association and University of Campinas. Campinas. Mimeo.

Meichtry, Norma Cristina. 1978. "Estrutura Geodemográfica de la Provincia de Corrientes." *Estudios Regionales,* no. 7. Centro de Estudios Regionales del Nordeste Argentino. Corrientes.

Mermel, T. W. 1987. "Major Dams of the World." *Water Power and Dam Construction. 1983.* Handbook, 43–50.

Murphy, Kathleen J. 1983. *Macroproject Development in the Third World. An Analysis of Transnational Partnerships.* Boulder: Westview Press.

Nash, June. 1979. "Anthropology of the Multinational Corporations." In *New Directions in Political Economy. An Approach from Anthropology*, edited by Madeline Barbara Leons and France Rothstein. Westport, Connecticut: Greenwood Press.

———. 1981. "Ethnographic Aspects of the World Capitalist System." *Annual Review of Anthropology* 10: 393–423.

Olien, Roger M., and Diana D. Olien. 1982. *Oil Booms: Social Change in Five Texas Towns.* Lincoln: University of Nebraska Press.

Palerm, Angel. 1973. *Obras Hidráulicas Prehispánicas en el Sistema Lacustre del Valle de México.* México: SEP-INAH.

Palerm, Angel & Vera Rubin, eds. 1959. *Plantation Systems of the New World.* Social Science Monograph 7. Washington: Pan American Union.

Panaia, Marta. 1985. *Los Trabajadores de la Construcción. Cambios y Evolución del Empleo en la Indústria de la Construcción Argentina.* Buenos Aires: Ediciones del IDES.

Partridge, William L., and Dennis Warren. 1984. "Introduction: Development Anthropology and the Life Cycle of Development Projects." In *Training Manual in Development Anthropology*, edited by W. Partridge. Special Publication of the American Anthropological Association and the Society of Applied Anthropology, no. 17.

Partridge, William L., Antoinette Brown, and Jeffrey Nugent. 1982. "The Papaloapan Dam and Resettlement Project: Human Ecology and Health Impacts." In *Involuntary Migration: The Problems and Responses of Dislocated People*, edited by Art Hansen and Anthony Oliver-Smith. Boulder: Westview Press.

Payer, Cheryl. 1982. *The World Bank: A Critical Analysis.* New York: Monthly Review Press.

Paz, Pedro. 1985. "Proceso de Acumulación y Política Económica." In *Crisis de la Dictadura Argentina. Política Económica y Cambio Social (1976–1983)*, edited by Eduardo Jozami, Pedro Paz, and Juan Villarreal. Buenos Aires: Siglo Veintiuno Editores.

Piore, Michael J. 1979. *Birds of Passage. Migrant Labor and Industrial Societies.* Cambridge: Cambridge University Press.

Pitkin, D. S. 1959. "The Intermediate Society: A Study in Articulation." In *Intermediate Societies, Social Mobility, and Communication*, edited by V. F. Ray. Proceedings of the Spring Meeting of the American Ethnological Society. Seattle.

Pitt-Rivers, J. A. 1954. *The People of the Sierra.* London.

Portes, Alejandro, and Robert L. Bach. 1985. *Latin Journey. Cuban and Mexican Immigrants in the United States.* Berkeley: University of California Press.

Provincia de Corrientes. 1978. *Relevamiento y Análisis de la Población Rural Bajo Cota 84 en la Provincia de Corrientes.* Ministério de Bienestar Social.

———. 1980a. *Relocalizaciones Rurales.* Ministério de Economia. Secretaría de Estado de Coordinación y Programación Económica. Oficina Coordinadora de Yacyretá, Corrientes.

———. 1980b. *Proyecto Ejecutivo Básico para la Relocalización de la Población Rural Bajo Cota 84 en la Provincia de Corrientes.* Ministério de Economia. Secretaría de Estado de Coordinación y Programación Económica. Oficina Coordinadora de Yacyretá, Corrientes.

———. 1981. *Caracterización Física Social y Económica del Area de Influencia de Yacyretá.* Ministério de Economia. Dirección de Planeamiento.

———. 1984. *Encuesta Sócio-Económica. Localidad: Ituzaingó.* Secretaría General de la Gobernación. Dirección de Estadísticas y Censos.

———. 1986. *Caracterización Sócio-Económica del Departamento de Ituzaingó.* Dirección de Planeamiento.

———. *Ituzaingó-Yacyretá. Guía Para Inversionistas.* Ministério de Economia.

Quijano, Aníbal. 1988. "Modernidad, identidad y utopía en América Latina." In *Imágenes Desconocidas. La Modernidad en la Encrucijada Postmoderna,* edited by Fernando Calderón. Buenos Aires: CLACSO.

Ratier, Hugo. 1971. *El Cabecita Negra.* Buenos Aires: Centro Editor de América Latina.

Revista Construcciones. 1985. "Complejo Yacyretá." *Construcciones,* no. 312 (Octubre): 2–32. Cámara Argentina de la Construcción.

Ribeiro, Darcy. 1970. *Os Indios e a Civilização. A Integração das Populações Indígenas no Brasil Moderno.* Petrópolis: Vozes.

Ribeiro, Gustavo Lins. 1980. "O Capital da Esperança. Brasília, um estudo sobre uma grande obra da construção civil." Master's Thesis. Graduate Program in Anthropology. University of Brasilia.

———. 1982. "Arqueologia de Uma Cidade. Brasília e suas Cidades Satélites." *Espaço e Debates* 5: 113–24.

———. 1985. "Proyectos de Gran Escala: Hacia un Marco Conceptual para el Análisis de una Forma de Producción Temporaria." In *Relocalizados: Antropología Social de las Poblaciones Desplazadas,* edited by Leopoldo J. Bartolomé. Buenos Aires: Ediciones del IDES.

———. 1987. "Cuanto Más Grande Mejor? Proyectos de Gran Escala: Una Forma de Producción Vinculada a la Expansión de Sistemas Económicos." *Desarrollo Económico* 105: 3–27.

———. 1990. "Latin America and the Development Debate." *Indian Journal of Social Science* 3(2): 271–95.

———. 1991. *Empresas Transnacionais. Um grande projeto por dentro.* São Paulo/Rio de Janeiro: Marco Zero/ANPOCS.

———. 1992. "Ambientalismo e Desenvolvimento Sustentado: Ideologia e Utopia no Final do Século XX." *Ciência da Informação* 21(1): 23–31.

Robertson, A. F. 1986. *People and the State. An Anthropology of Planned Development.* Cambridge: Cambridge University Press.

Rofman, Alejandro B. 1983. *Monetarismo y Crisis en el Nordeste.* Buenos Aires: Ediciones CEUR.

Rofman, Alejandro B., and Luís A. Romero. 1973. *Sistema Sócioeconómico y Estructura Regional en la Argentina.* Buenos Aires: Amorrortu Editores.

Rofman, Alejandro, A. Quintar, N. Marques, and Mabel Manzanal. 1987. *Políticas Estatales y Desarrollo Regional. La Experiencia del Gobierno Militar en la Región del NEA (1976–1981).* Buenos Aires: Ediciones CEUR.

Rojas, Isaac Francisco et al. *Una Geopolítica Nacional Desintegrante.* Buenos Aires: Nemont Ediciones, 1980.

Romero, José Luís. 1986. *Breve História de la Argentina.* 7th ed. Buenos Aires: Editorial Abril.

Schreiber, Janet M. 1975. "Ethnicity as a Factor in Italian Temporary Worker Migration." In *Migration and Urbanization: Models of Adaptive Strategies,* edited by Brian M. du Toit and Helen Safa. The Hague-Paris: Mouton Publishers.

Scudder, Thayer, and Elizabeth Colson. 1982. "From Welfare to Development: a Conceptual Framework for the Analysis of Dislocated People." In *Involuntary Migration and Resettlement. The Problems and Responses of Dislocated People,* edited by Art Hansen & Anthony Oliver-Smith. Boulder: Westview Press.

Sigaud, Lygia. 1986. "Efeitos Sociais de Grandes Projetos Hidroelétricos. As Barragens de Sobradinho e Machadinho." *Comunicação,* no. 9. Museu Nacional. Rio de Janeiro.

Silverman, Sydel F. 1965. "Patronage and Community-Nation Relationships in Central Italy." *Ethnology,* 172–89.

Steward, Julian H. 1950. "Sociocultural Wholes as Integrative Levels." *Area Research. Social Science Research Council Bulletin,* no. 63: 106–14.

———. 1955. *Theory of Culture Change.* Urbana: University of Illinois Press.

———. 1979. "Levels of Sociocultural Integration: An Operational Concept." In *Theory of Cultural Change. The Methodology of Multilinear Evolution.* Urbana: University of Illinois Press.

Summa, Revista de Arquitectura, Tecnología y Diseño. October 1984. Buenos Aires.

Szentes, Tamás. 1988. *The Transformation of the World Economy. New Directions and New Interests.* London: Zed Books.

Szuchman, Mark D. 1980. *Mobility and Integration in Urban Argentina. Cordoba in the Liberal Era.* Austin: University of Texas Press.

Tilly, Louise. 1985. "Coping with Company Paternalism: Family Strategies of Coal Miners in Nineteenth-Century France." *Theory and Society* 14: 403–17.

Velho, Otávio Guilherme. 1972. *Frente de Expansão e Estrutura Agrária.* Rio de Janeiro: Zahar.

———. 1976. *Capitalismo Autoritário e Campesinato.* São Paulo: Difel.

Vitale, Luís. 1986. *História de la Deuda Externa Latinoamericana y Entretelones del Endeudamiento Argentino.* Buenos Aires: Sudamericana-Planeta.

Wallerstein, Immanuel. 1974. *The Modern World-System. Capitalist Agriculture and the Origins of the European World-Economy in the Sixteenth Century.* New York and London: Academic Press.

Wittfogel, Karl A. 1957. *Oriental Despotism. A Comparative Study of Total Power.* New Haven: Yale University Press.

Wolf, Eric R. 1956. "Aspects of Group Relations in a Complex Society: Mexico." *American Anthropologist* 58: 1065–78.

———. 1982. *Europe and the People Without History.* Berkeley: University of California Press.

# Index